To Miranda,
Happy Days and Happy Horses
from
Mozzy D

A Reckless Ride

TONY DAMPIER

authorHOUSE®

AuthorHouse™ UK Ltd.
500 Avebury Boulevard
Central Milton Keynes, MK9 2BE
www.authorhouse.co.uk
Phone: 08001974150

© 2007 Tony Dampier. All rights reserved.

No part of this book may be reproduced, stored in a retrieval system, or transmitted by any means without the written permission of the author.

First published by AuthorHouse 10/12/2007

ISBN: 978-1-4343-0519-0 (sc)
ISBN: 978-1-4343-0520-6 (hc)

Printed in the United States of America
Bloomington, Indiana

This book is printed on acid-free paper.

To my lovely girls. Ann, Nicki, Jenny, Becky, Jacqueline, Clare, Dominique and the boys. Matthew, Adam, Richard, Rohan and Jimmy.

Above all, the Queen Bee.

My Wife 'B' riding 'Notario'

FORWARD
BY SILVIA STANIER L.V.O.

When I first read the text of Tony Dampier's book, I thought, Goodness this is a breath of fresh air! So many books are only concerned with teaching one to ride.

Like myself Tony has travelled the world – which in itself is interesting - He has been fortunate enough to find horses along the way which have been both unusual and in some cases, unfortunate. This has taught him to look at horses as individuals and as friends. This is a lesson to all of us, and what satisfaction Tony has got out of this.

I recommend anyone interested in horses, especially their welfare to read this book.

Silvia Stanier L.V.O.

INTRODUCTION

These stories spring from a life time of working with horses. I consider myself blessed that I have been able to devote my working life to something I feel so passionately about, enjoying every minute spent in the company of horses.

Every horse can teach so much to its handler if that handler takes the time to listen and observe. Also, as riders, we cannot and must not attempt to work outside of the nature of the horses entrusted to us. Understanding and respecting the horses nature allows it to express itself in its work, sometimes quite brilliantly. This also helps us to work in physical, mental, emotional and spiritual balance which we can carry forward into our daily lives.

I often think that the three golden words in classical training, Calm, Forward and Straight, are a pretty good philosophy for life.

The horses in this book are the unsung heroes of the horse world. They have not been the gatherers of glittering prizes but by honest toil and great personality led good lives, helped a little, I like to think, by my efforts but more often the opposite was the case.

These then are the tales of only a few of the many hundreds of horses I have been involved with. There are many more tales to be told and , God willing, many more horses for me to meet.

The book is not my story, it is the animals story. If most of the human characters in these pages appear as mere shadows, I make no apology, for they are only the bit players, the horses are the stars.

The First Of Many
Chapter 1

The old Clydesdale mare stretched contentedly in her deep bed of wheat straw, enjoying the luxury of the warm comfort of her stall and listened to the scurrying of fat mice, disturbed from their nightly feasting on stolen grain. Yawning, she decided that it was time to get up. She had no trouble getting to her feet within the confines of her stall. The heavy, wooden bobbin on the end of her head rope rose with her. She stretched each back leg out behind her, drew her chin into her breast, arching her thick neck and so prepared herself for the day ahead.

She tapped a hind hoof on the side of the elegantly curved boskin that separated her from her best buddy as though to tell him that it was time to wake up. The little grey gelding on the other side of the partition was already on his feet, snuffling through the straw in search of any scraps of grain that the robber mice had missed in there nocturnal scavenging, at the same time keeping one ear cocked towards the stable door in anticipation of his morning feed.

The boskin prevented the horses seeing each other but that didn't matter, they could feel each other's presence in their quiet breathing and the whispering of the crisp, yellow straw beneath there feet.

Before first light, the stable door swung open and they blinked like wise old owls at the sudden brightness as the stable light snapped on. A familiar friendly voice told them to move over as a bucket of fresh water was carried into each stall, to be followed by a feed of rolled oats, broad flaked bran and chopped straw.

Later, when the farmer went indoors to breakfast, my brother David and I arrived at the farm to lovingly brush the horses soft, sweet smelling coats in readiness for the days work. Is there anything that smells as wholesome as a horse?

Blossom; the dark bay Clydesdale, stood at well over 16.2 hands high, with feet like dinner plates hidden beneath a wealth of white, silky feathering. Silver; her friend, on the other hand, was a fifteen-hand grey gelding of a 'certain age' and a more refined ancestry, being lighter of bone with a fine head and the high tail carriage of an Arabian horse. Silver's cheeky outlook on life was a constant embarrassment to the more level-headed Blossom who often rewarded the greys unbecoming behaviour with a nip on his hindquarters.

'Blossom' with my brother David (Sam)

Never had two horses had so much loving attention lavished upon them as this pair. My brothers, Jim and David and I polished and groomed them every day of the school holidays. Blossom's coat was burnished to a high gloss and dapples of good health covered her hindquarters, whilst Silver could have advertised Persil washing powder, to which he owed much of his cleanliness. The harness gleamed where the leather was still good and the rusty, work worn chains and collar hames were well oiled. The harness was really in dreadful condition, but it was all we had and it did the job, fitting where it touched, with any necessary repairs done on the spot with lengths of hairy binder twine.

The two horses were devoted to each other and bonded to the point where it became impossible to work one out of sight of the other. Blossom particularly, would fret, shout and break into a muck-sweat on the rare occasions that the two were parted.

Although tractors were in plentiful supply, old Paul, the farmer, never did get round to purchasing one, all the equipment on the farm was horse drawn, consequently, Blossom and Silver had to work hard for their corn. They cut the sweet smelling meadow hay with a loud chattering mower that caused hares to run in panic and skylarks to sing their neurotic way to the heavens. They turned the hay to let the wind and sun dry it before stooking it in bundles ready to be pulled out of the fields on the huge, creaking hay wagon and into the barn, where it was unloaded. Hay seemed to make better when it was stacked loose in the barn, rather than baled tightly with little or no air passing through it. I remember that it kept its sweet smell all winter long.

Hay making and corn harvesting were enchanted times for us youngsters. Days of endless sunshine, bread and cheese and bottles of "Dandelion and Burdock" while the golden Labradors lay like honey melting in the noonday sun, far too contented and lazy to make the effort to chase rabbits and hares. Together with the all pervading nut brown smell of sweating horses and the chance of a stolen kiss under the hay cart from the prettiest of the girls who came to help, how we wished those days would never end. We would stay at the farm until the raggedy winged crows were homeward bound in the purple evening light.

It was during hay making time (the last at Oak Bank Farm it turned out) that Brother David and I took our revenge on a neighbouring farmer who had reneged on an agreement to pay us for lifting potatoes, a backbreaking job for which we should never have volunteered. He lived on his own, his wife; a fearsome creature, who was all God and pew rough knees had left him ten summers ago because it was rumoured, she feared his desire to have too frequent biblical knowledge of her. And so the lonely, bitter farmer had no one to bring his lunch out to him at noon and usually made his weary way up to his tumble down house to eat, leaving his old, neglected mare "Dolly", unshod, and broken footed, harnessed up in the field with neither food nor water.

For two days, we patiently bided our time until our potential victim was working the lower end of his land. Here, the horse and wagon would be hidden from the enemy's view. At 12.30 pm Dolly was left on her own. We allowed a few minutes to pass before sending the youngest of our group crawling through the grass to the top of the rise to act as lookout, whilst the rest of us set about unyoking Dolly to lead her out through the five-barred gate and onto the lane. We then pushed the shafts of the wagon between the bars of the old oak gate and re-yoked Dolly. After retreating a safe distance we awaited the return of our cheating farmer. Instead of the show of anger we had expected the poor chap was quite puzzled and sat down on the cart whilst he tried to work out how his horse had managed to get herself in such a predicament.

Not all the work was hard for Silver and Blossom. Their day started by delivering milk in the Whitefield area, north of Manchester. It was a small round, just enough for Paul to get through on his own, now that he was getting on a bit. He was a good man, hard-working; cheerful and extremely kind, with a face like a dry stonewall and a voice as mellow as well used leather. We loved working with him.

Blossom and Silver worked side by side in the milk float. Blossom; between the shafts, did the actual work with Silver tied to the offside of her collar to keep the mare company and avoid us having to put up with her noisy and moody behaviour if her friend was left at home.

Dressed in a weird assortment of harness, complimented with string and wire, where necessary to allow for the great difference in size and shape between the Clydesdale and the pony, we would set off on the round early in the morning. If it wasn't hard work for Blossom it was even easier for Silver, who quite rightly believed he was only coming along for the walk and to greet his public as they came out to pay homage with gifts of carrots, apples and slices of bread. Totally lacking in manners, he grabbed the proffered titbit like a starving dog, as though afraid that it might disappear. Blossom on the other hand took her share as gently and carefully as a child taking the Eucharist at its first Communion. To us children this pair of horses were the most beautiful creatures on earth. Alas, when I recently came across an old photograph of them I realized that they were exceedingly plain to look at, but oh, how they were loved

A Reckless Ride

The pair of horses knew the daily milk round as well as old Paul did. They knew where to stop, where to go on again and even understood the traffic signals on the main Manchester road. All this made life easier for the old man, but he still allowed us to go along with him to help. I think he got a laugh from our antics as we vied with each other to make deliveries. One of us would race to bring milk jugs from the doorsteps, whilst another would plunge the dipper into the churn of foaming milk, ready to fill the jugs. This was before milk bottles were used. The best worker of the day had the privilege of driving the horses back home and Old Paul made sure that we each had a fair share of being the best worker. Once young hands took the reins imagination flew like birds, John Wayne's stagecoach, Ben Hurr's chariot and the Deadwood stage were all busy in Whitefield during those long summer holidays.

As people became a little more affluent in the years following the war the farm's horse population began to grow. First to arrive was Flicka, a black cob mare, next came a bay thoroughbred named Gay, this was before the word was hijacked and given a less wholesome meaning. Others followed and I was given the glorious opportunity of riding most of them in return for helping to paint stables (black at the bottom up to four feet, and white above), mucking out, grooming and taking horses to the farrier's shop on Poppythorn Lane. At the smithy, the number of vehicles parked outside allowed us to estimate waiting time. All this was done with the feeling of being privileged to handle the horses with no thought of monetary gain.

The farriers shop became a sanctuary for wounded ex- service men returning from the war who were unable to find the promised work in this land fit for heroes. Soldiering has always been an honourable profession when there is a war to be fought. The soldiers are fondly referred to as "Our boys" but when the war is won and we can all sleep safely in our beds again, no one wants to know them. They are little more than an embarrassment.

Unknowingly I learned a great deal from those horses, particularly about balance and feel as I very rarely had access to a saddle. I knew nothing of dressage or any other discipline; Any knowledge I had came from ancient, pre-war copies of Horse and Hound and the racing columns of the Daily Express, from which I clipped any pictures of horses I could find.

It was about this time, the late forties and early fifties, that the railways were killing off their horses in a mad rush to go mechanised. It was nothing less than sinful, thousands of fit young horses were slaughtered in the name of progress, but there we are, big business has never been a grateful employer.

I only mention this shameful episode in our history because it made available tons of equipment, most of which was broken up for the various metals and salvageable timber, but some made its way to the few farms that still used horses and in this way Blossom acquired a new set of harness and I acquired my first piece of horse furniture, a straight bar bit. It was a truly prized possession and hung on my bedroom wall to be gazed at and weave dreams around as I listened to my father's tales of greathorses and equestrian achievements.

With the help of a little girl friend who was as mad about horses as I was, I soon fashioned a bridle out of webbing and we set out to widen our equestrian experience.

Norma and I were the worst horse thieves in the county. Night after night we slipped our bridles onto grazing horses and rode beneath the stars to our hearts content. (Actually, that is not quite true; it was more often than not pouring down with rain.) Of course if I caught anyone doing the same to my horses I would show them no mercy.

My younger brother David with whom I shared many of these adventures, was known as Sam because Dad thought David was a Jewish name and the child might as well be named Samuel. Not that it made much difference to the old man; he couldn't remember any of the names of his nine children anyway and addressed us all as Charlie. We lads didn't mind at all but my sisters found it a little annoying.

One September morning, during a half term holiday, Sam and I arrived at the farm in good time to bring in the horses from the misty, silent field and harness up for the day's milk deliveries. There was an unnatural quietness about the place, even the aged toothless dog on its chain seemed subdued, ignoring the suicidal sheep hunched up in the corner of the yard, the chickens were still locked in their coops, dreaming their fear filled dreams, as chickens do.

A Reckless Ride

We stood around waiting for Mr Cropper to put in an appearance but to no avail, and so I bullied Sam to go and knock on the the big oak door. Eventually the door grated and creaked open letting a little light into the gloomy, tobacco stained interior. To our surprise a stranger in a long black coat and with an equally long face stood before us. He peered at Sammy over the top of his NHS spectacles with obvious disapproval and then at me hovering cowardly in the background, with equal disdain. He sniffed his specks up the bridge of his nose, before asking what we wanted. Sam stammered asort of village idiot explanation about the necessity of starting the milk round and our need of old Paul.

The stranger disappeared into the dark, St Bruno scented house and returned with a message, Would we please take the morning delivery ourselves, Mr Cropper died last night. Thank you. A bleak short announcement, telling us not only of the death of Paul Cropper, but in so many ways the passing of our childhood.

The milk round took a long, slow silent time to complete that day. Neither of us having the courage to speak of Paul's death, as if not speaking of it would make it not have happened. Yet the silent dread of the reality made us slow down in an attempt to delay the inevitable. We continued to go to the farm to help Mrs Cropper when we could, but the new-found responsibility came hard to dispirited young shoulders. Of course, it was much harder for the widow and within a few months, she told us that the farm was to be sold for housing development.

The last time I saw Blossom she had broken out of her retirement field and backed herself up to the shafts of the old hay cart waiting, as old people do, for who knows what? Silver fared better, he had been sold on as a riding horse to a very smart yard where he lived for many years. I like to think that he found another Blossom to torment in his new home.

Well; its all gone now, under a housing estate and the M62, yet there is a gentle reminder of these two horses forever on Oak Lane where a deep depression in the old dirt road, that required Blossom and Silver to be urged on to greater effort, was tarmac over to make a fast road to nowhere in particular. The depression is still there and I find myself silently calling out whenever I drive my car over it 'Come on Blossom, come on Silver'.

Guard Royal
Chapter 2

It was 1951 and at fifteen years of age, I left school. Got my first pair of long trousers and set about job hunting. Time available to spend with horses was reduced drastically. Earning one's keep was what life was all about. Education for what would now be referred to as our socio-economic group or some such, in those far off days, had been merely a preparation for work. The lads were expected to go into engineering apprenticeships or down the pit, while girls found jobs in the mills or shops, the bright ones becoming secretaries; if they were lucky, until it was their time to marry and produce more fodder for the factories and coal mines.

My brother Jim, like myself, did not wish to conform to the accepted way and he got himself apprenticed to the local farrier on Poppythorn lane in Prestwich. I also was more fortunate than most and was taken on as a trainee with a local photographer and, although I quite enjoyed the work, it was not for me, I wanted to be with horses but there were fewer opportunities now that horses were becoming redundant. In addition, employers were reluctant to take on young lads who would be disappearing into the army within a few months to do their National Service.

Rather than waiting for my call up papers and risk being sent to some infantry regiment for eighteen months, I signed on as a regular soldier in the Household Cavalry. Accepted the Queen's shilling and at seventeen years of age, I nervously took myself off to Hyde Park Barracks in London.

The moment I walked into the famous old stable yard at Knightsbridge I knew I had done the right thing. Never had I seen such glamour, such pride or such wonderful horses. I ached to be a part of it and I could hardly contain my impatience for training to begin at Combermere Barracks in Windsor, innocent that I was.

The Household Cavalry dismount after Trooping of the Colour 1955

I had expected the training to be tough, The Household Cavalry being the senior regiment of the Brigade of Guards with its legendary discipline, as befits an elite corps, but it was much harder than I had anticipated. The days were long and the parade ground hard on my country boy feet. My fellow recruits and I were taught to drill as only members of the Brigade of Guards can. Shoot Lee Enfield 3.03 rifles like snipers, these rifles had recoil like the kick of an angry mule and could dislocate your shoulder if not held firmly. We disguise ourselves as trees in open fields. We threw hand grenades as though we were playing cricket and almost killed ourselves on assault courses and cross-country runs. We learned by heart the language of the cavalry bugle calls 'Reveille', Feed away', 'Boots and saddles', and the hauntingly beautiful 'Last Post' played in the late evening as my comrades and I dropped wearily onto our hard, lumpy beds, I loved every minute of it, in retrospect.

After or passing out parade we were transferred to the Equitation wing under the eagle eye of Major Tommy Thompson. To us recruits, this Olympic equestrian was a God; we were in awe of him. Our instructors were all good horsemen who had proved themselves in competition, on the hunting field and in battle. Corporal of Horse Snaky White particularly impressed me, he was everything a cavalryman should be, tall, slim and dashing with all the time in the world to explain his art to an interested pupil. We all tried to model ourselves on Corporal of Horse, Snaky White.

The horses used in the riding school at that time were mostly rejects from Hyde Park Barracks having been deemed unsuitable for ceremonial duties, looking back, I am sure that most were unsuitable for anything other than teaching cocky young Lifeguards a little humility. These cavalry blacks could quickly sort the men from the boys. In the riding school, they could buck a rider up to the rafters, rear and pose on one hind leg for what seemed like hours at a time and they all enjoyed the sound and feel of a rider's leg being crushed and dragged along the school walls. It was a great relief to be assigned one of the more tolerant horses such as the gentle Devonian or Loppy Lemburgh, a well-behaved gelding that had spent his early days in a German cavalry regiment before being classified as spoils of war and brought to London. Eventually we came to an understanding with our mounts and were able to ride them in basic movements such as shoulder in and half pass as well as cavalry drill movements in sections of four and half sections of two, with four reins in the left hand and a sword in the right. We were taught to mount and dismount at the gallop, to ride down a jumping lane with neither stirrups nor reins and pluck a tent peg out of the ground with the point of a lance whilst galloping. Of course, we all prayed that we would draw one of the less psychotic animals for these forays into madness. It was great fun and after six weeks of intensive training, the wonderful day arrived when we were allowed to have stirrups. I often wonder what those dreadful, politically correct, Health 'n' Safety zealots would have made of it all,

Of course, it was not all about riding. Mucking out, grooming, tack cleaning to a very high standard and lectures took up a large part of the day as did dismounted cavalry drill and sword drill. Hour after hour, we were drilled in all the movements that we could expect to encounter on the streets of London during ceremonial occasions, until we were considered worthy enough to mount up and put to the test all that we had learned.

On Saturday mornings, the riding hall was reserved for loose jumping. Obstacles would be set out alongside the walls and the horses brought in one by one to jump without the unsympathetic weight of a rider on the end of the reins. This helped the horses' to regain their self-confidence and encourage them to think about what they were doing. If we had performed well throughout the week, we recruits were allowed to climb aboard and go over the jumps with neither reins nor saddle. Our balance, feel and confidence grew enormously, as did our visits to regimental medical officer.

At the conclusion of our training, those of us who had survived took part in a passing out parade where we were able to show off our new-found skills in front of the Commanding officer and other regimental dignitaries. Grand speeches were made and we were presented with our spurs, at last, we were trained cavalrymen. Or so we thought.

After a few days leave, we reported to our London barracks in Knightsbridge to begin training all over again, this time on better-behaved horses. Piece by piece we were introduced to the glamorous ceremonial uniform until we were familiar with riding in it and, just as importantly, cleaning it to an incredibly high standard. This included thigh boots, white gauntlets and buckskin breeches, tight tunics, scarlet for the Life Guards, blue for The Royal Horse Guards (a mounted squadron of each made up The Household Cavalry Regiment) and restricting cuirasses, topped off with a precariously balanced silver helmet and plume and a cavalry sabre swinging at our left hip.

The horse furniture, that is bits, styrups and the bright chain that is worn around the horses neck, required burnishing every day as did our swan neck spurs. the chain was placed in a sack with a lump of lead and swung around our heads to clean it. Next we placed the chain between the blankets of our beds believing that this would help to keep the shine fresh.

Sixteen weeks later, we passed out ready to take our place on ceremonial duties as part of the Sovereigns escort on grand state occasions and Guard duties at Horseguards in Whitehall. It would be

A Reckless Ride

easy to imagine that the Household Cavalry was purely a ceremonial regiment but nothing could be further from the truth. Men seen on parade today in all their finery astride the beautiful black horses will most likley be fighting in some God forsaken place like Afganistan or Iraq in a few weeks.

Behind the scenes all was not glamour Horses still needed looking after and exercising. If we were not on guard duty that day, after feeding and mucking out, we would give the horses a quick brush down, known as quartering, tack up our two horses for exercise and riding one and leading the other on our near side, would ride out as a troop around the still dark streets of London. Considering that the horses were each fed five pounds of oats per day, they usually behaved very well on exercise. We soon got use to riding in the dark city as all rehearsals for the Trooping of the Colour, Sovereigns escorts and escorts for foreign dignitaries were carried out at three or four am. On returning to barracks, we turned our horses in and were allowed to go to breakfast.

Things had not been going well for the mounted squadrons of The Household Cavalry. The Suez crisis of 1956 caused by the sudden Nationalization of the Suez Canal by President Nasser of Egypt and the over reaction of the British Government had restricted the regiment's activities and, in common with any military establishment on standby, boredom had set in. In more settled times the highlight of the year would have been Trooping the Colour on Horse guards Parade to celebrate Her Majesty the Queen's birthday. Another event popular with the troops was the famous Musical ride. To be selected for the ride was an honour and a chance to get out of the routine of barrack life for the duration of the show season plus the possibility of trips to Europe, Canada or America. All such things, including the popular summer camp at Pirbrite, were cancelled for 1956.

It was a summer of petty squabbles and a general lowering of standards among the troopers and NCOs. Eventually complaints from the Whitehall brass began to arrive in the Adjutant's office, sloppy behaviour, poor turnout and talking to the public, he was less than pleased.

The Adjutant at that time was a charming good-humoured man when things went well, but any sign of tardiness in his beloved

Tony Dampier

The Household Cavalry Musical Ride. 1955

regiment would result in skin and hair flying, or worse. A sure sign that this gentleman was upset was when he started to stammer and twitch; this affliction had earned him the nickname of Nodder.

Incensed by the incoming criticism from his superiors, Nodder decided to take The Queen's Guard himself. He would ride down the Mall in front of the finest troops mounted on the best cavalry blacks available. He would show the critics what the Household Cavalry was all about. A horse inspection was duly held in the stable yard of Knightsbridge barracks and the Adjutant made his selection of mounts for the guard. Selecting horses for The Queen's Guard is usually the prerogative of the troop NCOs, after all they know the characteristics of the animals in their troop and their suitability for a particular job or rider far better than most of the Officers did , but so mighty was the fury of the Adjutant, that none of the four troop leaders thought it politic to advise him on the selection of horses. One of the chosen animals was a handsome young gelding who had just joined the squadron from the Remount depot where he had shown great promise as a possible officer's charger, being rather finer bred than the type used as troop horses. This was to be Guard Royal`s first outing as a ceremonial troop horse and looked upon the whole thing in amazement.

All went well during the dismounted inspection, apart from poor Neddy Crapp who, when asked his name by the Adjutant, nerv-

A Reckless Ride

ously twitched, stammered and shouted out 'Crapp' at the top of his voice. His feet never touched the ground on his way to the lock-up.

Guard Royal stood like a rock; his heart pounding as the trumpeter sounded the Walk March. He wheeled to the right with the three other horses of his section, Mickey, Gartree Hill and the mighty Soda, Soda was a bit of a glamour boy being over seventeen hands high, with four sable marked white socks and a lovely, even blaze down his face. He took pride of place as the carrier of the Royal Standard and was very aware of his status taking on a military baring as soon as he was tacked up. The higher the rank of his rider the prouder he carried himself. In this august company Guard Royal marched through the barrack gates and onto Hyde Park Road to make his first appearenc in public.

Up until the 1970s, the Queen's Guard used to ride under the gateway at Hyde Park Corner on their way to Horse guards, via Constitution Hill and The Mall. As we passed under The arch of Hyde Park Corner a catalogue of disasters were set in motion when the wonderful underground railway system thoughtlessly scheduled one of its trains to pass under the arch just as Guard Royal was arriving there. The gallant young horse felt the strange vibrations under his iron-shod feet, rolled his eyes, snorted and shot off across the road towards Green Park. He leapt the low railings into the park and galloped across the pampered turf, scattering tourists and city folk alike, with two mounted police officers hot on his heels. Guard Royals rider; Trooper Jackson, clung on; as best he could in full state dress, he had lost his sword when the horse jumped the railings and a few strides later, his helmet and plume disappeared in the greensward of the park as the pair headed for Piccadilly circus. Fortunately they didn't make it and were `arrested` by the mounted police officers who returned horse, rider, helmet and sword to the detachment just in time for the Royal salute at Buckingham Palace.

As we passed the Palace, the Adujant, rather over enthusiasticly, bawled out at the top of his voice "Carry swords, eyeees right". With a swish of plumes and thump of sword hilts on sheepskin saddle covers the command was instantly obeyed. The trumpeter began to sound the salute, The trembling Guard Royal was beside himself and sweating profusely, he quite liked a little music in the stable but this noise so close to his ears was too much and he made another break for freedom. He barged into the trumpeter's grey horse like a polo pony, causing it to throw up its head, ramming the trumpet into the musicians mouth, knocking out two of his teeth and giving him a fat lip. This time the terrified horse galloped all the way down the Mall to Horse Guards Parade and skidded under the archway before sliding to a stop in the Tilt yard , a full ten minutes ahead of schedule, where the Royal Horse Guards were lined up waiting for the troop of The Life Guards to relieve them of their guard duties, where he waited, puffing and blowing, for his friends to arrive.

This was not to be the end of the Adjutant's nightmare. By the time they joined Guard Royal, the poor chap was beside himself, he was visibly shaking and his dreadful twitch became a very pronounced nod. This was bad enough, but cavalry, commands such as 'return swords' and 'dismount' are followed by a nod of the head, on which the order is carried out. Nodder was nodding like a drinking hen, troopers were returning swords to scabbards, mounting and dismounting, totally out of control.

Guard Royal had had enough, he waited until Trooper Jackson was standing on the nearside stirrup, about to step down and then gave an almighty buck, throwing the unfortunate soldier over his back to the offside and made his way into the stable yard where the rider was unhooked from his left stirrup and lowered to the ground.

The outcome of what was to become known as the 'Adjutant's Balls Up' was that on release from the lock-up, Trooper Jackson was put back into the recruits ride for sixteen weeks where he again caused problems by allowing his horse to jump over the six foot high riding school doors where; on landing, he dismounted without permission. We all felt some sympathy towards Jackson he was a better than average horseman and well liked, unfortunately he had drawn a few short straws, it could have been any one of us although secretly we were glad it wasn't.

Shortly after this episode, I achieved one of my modest goals by getting an unofficial job helping the remount staff, training horses for the regiment. Although the work was extremely enjoyable, it was hard going and had to be fitted around ceremonial duties. I was also looking after an officers charger, so in effect I had three jobs. The first horse I was asked to help with was the by now notorious, Guard Royal. He was given to me for rehabilitation. I think I got him because I was perhaps, the only rider daft enough to take him on.

The horse showed no signs of distress from his experiences and misadventures on the streets of London and it was not long before I was riding him out in Hyde Park every day. His particular delight was a Saturday morning hack to the Portobello Road market. Here the stallholders fed him apples and carrots by the bucketful and spoiled him dreadfully while I chatted to my girlfriend as she helped her dad on his stall.

Guard Royal was hard work in the riding hall needing a lot of encouraging leg pressure to get even a modestly rounded outline from him. He perked up when jumps were erected and he enjoyed popping over them; perhaps later he could join the Regimental jumping team if he continued to show a talent for it. Whenever possible I would school him outdoors in the Park. Here he was full of impulsion and expression, his energy went through his body into my hand, and he felt like a different horse.

I liked to work him long and low for the first fifteen minutes to rid him of any tension in his loins and allowing him to develop swing in his back. Concentrating on rhythm regardless of tempo I found that he soon began to lower his head to seek a contact with my friendly hand, at first he was a little hollow on the right, but with some persuasion from my left leg he quickly stretched into my right hand and straightened himself. Regardless of the difficulty of the exercise I hoped to ride, I never failed to use this routine of rhythm, contact, swing and straightness with him. Of course I encountered problems that with my limited experience I was unable to solve, but fortunately, help of the very best was at hand in the form of riders from the Spanish Riding School in Vienna, who were visiting the UK to perform at the Royal International Horse Show. The world famous white Lipizzaner horses were stabled with my regiment at Knightsbridge during this time and I took full advantage of the situation.

I couldn't keep away from these wonderful horses; I prowled the stables in the evenings, befriending riders and grooms alike, I sneaked into the riding hall every morning to watch the training sessions, and I saw for the first time horses that appeared to be unhindered by gravity. Floating in the elegant passage, leaving the earth in the powerful school leaps and moving in perfect harmony with their oh so quiet riders. How I longed to discover what secrets led to such art. Later I would attempt some of the exercises with Guard Royal and Empress, the officer's charger I was looking after, much to the amusement of my new friends. Of course I got it all wrong, but eventually advice took the place of fun poking and I absorbed everything like blotting paper.

The wisest advice I was given came from a rather autocratic, softly spoken gentleman whom I later learned was Colonel Podhijsky, the Director of the Spanish Riding School, He told me to always be prepared to listen to the horse, observe its character, to be guided by what I learned and felt and not to rush. Chief Rider George Wahl taught me the importance of a correct seat and its influence on the horse, I was also shown something of in-hand work where the horse, held on a short rein, performs high school movements without the weight of a rider. At the time I was unaware of what great men of influence these were in the world of classical riding, perhaps if I had realised I would not have been so forward. As it was we accepted each other as fellow horsemen and got along well. Sadly, it was one of our own who chased me away from the Lipizzaners whenever he caught me near them. The fierce Corporal Major, Jock Ferrie, a brilliant horseman who later went on to train the Irish Olympic Teams. During the few weeks that the Spanish Riding School was with us, I incurred his wrath several times a day and went back for more. I was so hungry for knowledge.

In time, Guard Royal became familiar with many advanced dressage movements. Not all performed well, we were both very inexperienced and a great many mistakes were made, but we were having a go. Sadly, I was not to partner him in any competitions as I had hoped to, A high ranking officer took a shine to him and I had no choice but to hand him over. From that day on his dressage ceased and he became a hunter for an unappreciative, rather pompous rider who took him to all the fashionable meets where the poor horse spent more time waiting in a flashy horsebox outside a pub or stately home than enjoying the chase.

Eventually the time came for me to transfer to the armoured section of the regiment, and I decided that it was time to move on. I remember feeling very sad as I bade a farewell to the Household Cavalry and the wonderful horses. I will be eternally grateful to the military horses I trained; These were my professors and they taught me so much, as all horses do.

BADGER
CHAPTER 3.

I found it difficult to settle down to a civilian way of life after all the glamour, the fine horses and the comradeship of the Cavalry. I tried a few boring jobs to earn a little money but I was restless to get back to working with horses and I eventually rented a small stable yard close to my home town of Bury where I set about building up a business in the horse industry. It was a long hard struggle but enthusiasm and a burning passion made it a labour of love.

In the boom years of the 1960s and 1970s when T V coverage of equestrian events was at an all time high, Great show jumping horses such as Foxhunter, The Quiet Man and Vibart became household names encouraging as it did, thousands of young people to take up riding and horse owning, my little business thrived. I was not prosperous enough to buy the expensive show jumpers or top flight dressage horses, these can command a king's ransom yet may never win a penny for their new owners (the dress rarely looks as good on the buyer as it did on the model).

Top competition horses are hardly ever sold and if such a horse came onto the market it would go; complete with rides at important shows, within hours, to a rider with insider knowledge and most likely a wealthy sponsor.

I went for the middle of the road horses that, because of some defect in behaviour or conformation, could be bought for a modest sum. Usually the problems that arise with horses are the results of poor training, rough schooling and ill treatment, or, as is more often the case, all three. However, with careful and sympathetic handling the problem can usually be eradicated to the point where the animal is once again a useful and attractive proposition to a potential buyer.

Buying and re-schooling these unfortunate animals was a good sideline in my riding school and livery business and I could double my money within a month or so. Any horse I could not sell with a good name went to the auction sales in Cheshire to be sold without warranty. On reflection I think it was these unfortunate animals that made me decide never to become a horse dealer.

One memorable horse I acquired was Badger, a handsome 16.2 hands, eight year old bay gelding. This was before the fashion for big, rather dull, continental animals took hold. Badger was one of the best looking horses that had ever come my way. Everything was in proportion with strong hindquarters to propel him forward, a short strong back and good length of rein. He absolutely boiled with presence. What a dream of a horse he was.

His history, as is usual with 'dodgy' horses, was lost in a fog of mystery. His owner knew little of Badger's past other than that he was related to the mighty Arkle and had won everything from the Grand National to an Olympic gold. In short, all the usual imaginative garbage that goes with a duff horse. Badger's lady owner had paid a lot of money for him on the assumption that if one paid enough the goods would be sound, poor dear. She wanted to send the horse to me for re-schooling. I must admit that I was not keen on undertaking the task as I had more than enough to do running a yard of 40 horses. However, always a sucker for a hard luck story and a pretty face , I took him on, on the understanding that if the horse did not improve within one month the lady was to take him away.

For the first few days Badger's impeccable, behaviour fooled me but as is the way with horses and humans, once settled into his new surroundings, he began to assert himself. Initially this took the form of violently kicking his stable door with a front leg at first light and keeping up the bombardment until he got his morning feed. This is not an uncommon vice and possibly has its origins in the hungry wild horse digging for roots or through snow for a bite of grass. Be that as it may, it is an annoying habit and it's not too good for stable doors either. The problem was reduced; if not solved, by stabling Badger as close to the feed store as possible so that he would be first in line for feeding. This of course was not without drawbacks, because every time anyone went near the feed store the blasted horse would start banging.

The real trouble began when I decided to take him out for a hack just to get the feel of him. We had got no more than a hundred yards from the stable yard when he stopped dead. I closed my legs strongly against his flanks to send him on, there was not a flicker of response. I let him feel my spurs, again nothing. Once more I put my legs on him and supported this with the whip, not very strongly, and gave a growl. Instant action, but in the wrong direction. Badger went up on his hind legs almost vertically. I grabbed his mane and clung on hoping that the damned fool horse wouldn't go over backwards. He did not, but as soon as he dropped his front legs to the ground, he started running backwards at an awesome speed until he backed us both into a ditch and down we went into the well rotted, slime and muck.

Fortunately, I managed to leap off the daft animals back before he could crash down on top of me but I still landed in the ditch. After an undignified scramble we were both on the road again and with the stupidity that comes from the unholy alliance of youth and arrogance I once more climbed into the saddle determined not to be beaten. What folly, for no sooner had my wet butt touched the saddle than the gormless animal went up again. This time he did lose his balance and crashed over onto his right buttock and my right leg. Enough was enough; I limped into the yard feeling very stupid, with a smug looking Badger in tow.

An hour and a few brandies later, changed and dry, but rather stiff, I again mounted Badger and rode out of the yard, this time behind two other horses and riders. What a superb ride this horse gave me. His paces were rhythmical, springy and balanced with an almost unbelievable suppleness and what a well educated mouth he had. We even popped over a few ditches and fallen logs. He felt good over these little obstacles and seemed to enjoy himself and so I invited him to jump one of the big, black , dry stone walls that criss cross the Pennines. Badger gathered himself and leapt effortlessly off his big hocks, rounding his back like the dome of St Paul's, beautiful. I realised that here was one hell of a horse if only I could cure him of his jibbing and rearing.

Often, if the cause of a problem can be found, one is half way towards solving it. Alas, all enquiries into the horse's past came to nought apart from the fact that he had come from Ireland 'about two years ago'. He had one season with the Cheshire Forest hounds and was then sold at Leicester sales as 'property of an officer going abroad' and knocked down to a north country dealer who in turn had sold him on to his present owner.

I racked my brains to find a solution to this wonderful horse's misdemeanour's. Perhaps he would respond to a little T.L.C? He got worse. Should I throw him down in the stable to show him that I could do anything I liked with him, but this horse loved lying down and allowed me to push and pull him around and roll him over, it was all great fun to him.

For the time being I decided only to ride him out in the company of other horses and we got on very well together, unless I asked him to take the lead, then he would threaten to rear. Badger's attitude towards the other horses when he was turned out in the paddock was surprisingly servile and he seemed to lack the ability to stand up for himself. He was devoid of any self-confidence whatsoever and this was possibly the root of his behavioural problems. He was the sort of horse that would never have survived in a natural state, living free. Badger was not and never would be a leader; not that this is a sin, in spite of the current philosophy that all men and beasts must be winners. In fact, the world is full of loveable losers and triers.

Badger did all he could to please. In the riding school, he learned quickly and well, he had energy to spare and it was too easy to produce more impulsion than either he or I could control resulting in some dramatic but undesirable acrobatics, Badger was also something of an innovator and would invent the most bizarre new dressage movements if I didn't keep my concentration. In the stable he was so well mannered that if he could talk he would have apologised for needing to be mucked out. I became rather fond of the silly horse and persuaded his owner to leave him with me a little longer. After all he had improved in so many ways, although I was still light years away from curing his vice of jibbing.

Misty October arrived with its usual melancholy moods and with autumn came the hunting season. Just the thing to give Badger some self-confidence I thought. He was half way to being fit and when he was clipped free of his winter coat he looked a million dollars and became quite cheeky. Putting in the occasional light-hearted buck in the morning. However, before arrangements had been made to take him to a meet the horse's owner phoned to ask me if I would buy him from her as she felt that she would never have the confidence to ride him again. To cut a long story short, Badger became mine for £300, which, oddly enough, was exactly the amount the fair lady owed me for his keep and schooling.

Our local hunt, the Holcomb Harriers, is said to be the oldest hunt in the country and were given the privilege of wearing Royal scarlet, rather than the green worn by other harrier packs by King James 1st after he had enjoyed a particularly good days sport with them. Legend has it, that at dinner on the same occasion the delighted King knighted the loin of beef, to be known forever as Sirloin.

One of the unwritten rules of hunting; and there are many, is that one never uses the hunting field for schooling young horses. However, being young and daft I told myself that I could handle any situation that might arise with my equally daft horse and was quite happy to break this rule without a troubled conscience. I believe that there is nothing better for teaching a young horse to look after itself than a few half days with hounds, and for Badger it worked wonders. One could feel this lovely horse's self-esteem growing in the enthusiastic way in which he greeted each new hunting morning. Oh, he knew what day it was without a doubt, with the changes in his routine, from plaiting his mane and tail the night before to the early start of activities on those lovely crisp mornings. We endeavoured to arrive at the meet in good time. As the Holcombe meet, uniquely, at twelve a.m. rather than the traditional eleven a.m. It gave us an extra hour to prepare and to leave things in good order at the stables. On arrival at a meet Badger would be so wound up that his coat would be dark with sweat with an almost manic look in his eye. Mounting demanded the athletic ability and control of a ballet dancer.

When hounds moved off the excited Badger would canter on the spot blowing and snorting like a steam engine until he took his place behind the more experienced horses. His performance in the field was exceptional, his self-control and eye for a stride made him a fast, safe ride and after his second day out he would quite happily take the lead over any fence, nor did he mind the hounds milling around his legs, not once did he offer to kick. On the two occasions that the Huntsman commandeered him, he was loath to return him to me so good was the ride he had been given

That year the winter turned vicious. Hunting was abandoned for the whole of January. The wind came screaming off the monochrome moor and whistled eerily between the rocks. Deformed oak trees swayed and leaned towards the naked earth as if looking for shelter. The days were short and the fox yelping nights were long. Trying to keep over-fresh horses with their seemingly glass legs, exercised on iron hard ground was fraught with dangers of slipping and jarred joints. We did all we could to keep horses in reasonable condition. Straw was spread deeply over the yard to hopefully prevent accidents, legs were bandaged and knee boots covered vulnerable joints. And then, quite suddenly, the weather softened and hunting recommenced with a meet at The Pack Horse Inn in Birtle, just half a mile from my yard . Within minutes of leaving the Pub, hounds found a hare and away we went in the direction of Buckhurst. Badger jumped the first dry stone wall rather cautiously but after that he was into his stride and flew the walls in good style. We had a great day and as a hare will always run in a circle we arrived back at the Pack Horse where we had started and home in time for evening stables.

Badger was always keen but he could be relied upon to behaved like an angel. Regretfully, he was starting to be noticed and a few tentative enquiries were being made regarding the possibility of buying him. One chap was keen to ride him in the "Mill workers Grand National" as the Holcombe Point to Point races was known but I was very reluctant to part with him until I felt confident that he was over his problem. It would have been very unfair to pass on such an unreliable horse. Eventually, towards the end of the season a super offer was made of an almost open cheque, provided the potential purchaser had a satisfactory, half-day trial, riding Badger to hounds. Arrangements were made for the gentleman to ride Badger at a meet of the Pendle and Craven Harriers . Naturally I was on pins awaiting their return home and was alarmed to see the potential client arrive back at my yard, without the horse. The most awful vision of my lovely Badger with a broken leg in some inaccessible Pennine ditch filled my head. Fortunately my fears were short lived and I was put out of my misery when I was told that Badger had given my client such a grand day that he had not taken the risk of bringing him back to my yard in case I changed my mind about selling him. The gentleman then asked me to name my price; this I did and without a quibble received over five times what I had paid for the horse.

    I was well pleased with my deal, but must confess to feeling a little envious when Badger was later sold to an international event rider for many times the price I had got for him. His new owner changed the horses name and later he changed hands again and was shipped out to America to continue his eventing career.

MAJOR
Chapter Four

It was a Manchester morning. A morning of incessant, soaking drizzle and sickly yellow light. Puddle-drenched office workers steamed in their dark-town rooms and shop assistants complained the same wet complaints of yesterday.

Across the damp old city at Ardwick Green, a simple but historic event was about to take place, an event that would mark the end of over a thousand years of the region's history. The last nine horses to work the streets of Manchester were about to go under the auctioneer's hammer.

During the late 19th and early 20th century this Victorian City employed the services of some 13,000 horses, all stabled within its precincts. Now in 1962 the horse population was down to this last nine. That all nine horses were Clydesdale was not surprising, these long striding animals were ideal for city work, being faster than a Shire horse and strong enough to draw a heavy workload. Often they worked in tandem to allow access to the narrow, cobbled back streets of old Manchester.

In common with all cities, Manchester had been built on the sweat of horses, every brick, piece of timber, cobble stone, glass windows and worker was carried by horse and when they had

Railway chain horses, Manchester c 1930

built the offices, shops and wear houses, they carried the merchandise to be sold. What a debt the the merchants of Manchester owe to the horse.

The horses to be sold that dull, grey day were kept at Hutchinson's, Globe stables, a functional if unimpressive range of buildings consisting of cart sheds, harness rooms, feed stores, wheelwright, saddler's' and farriers' shops, these were all situated on the ground floor, whilst on the upper floor were the stables. The stables were made up of large stalls with solid oak partitions where the horses were secured by a rope passing through their manger, situated beneath wooden hay racks and fastened to an oak bobbin that was just heavy enough to take up the slack when the horse moved forward, thus reducing the risk of a front leg being caught over the rope. There were no automatic water bowls to grace the stalls in those days. The occupants were led out three times a day to huge water troughs to drink their fill, under the supervision of the horse keeper, usually an ex cavalryman who was responsible for the welfare of the horses and their day's work allocation.

It was from stables such as this; in the seventeen and eighteen hundreds, that one hundred or so pack horse trains of twenty animals or more would leave Manchester for Liverpool each day, travelling along what is now the East Lancashire Road (A580) with just as many animals making their way to Manchester from Liverpool.

Every year on the first of May, the official birthday of all horses, except thoroughbreds who share January 1st as an official birthday, these grand working animals would be dressed with their best harness, polished to a mirror finish. Chain work that had been placed in sacks with a lump of lead and fastened to the wheels of the carts for days before, shone like new silver. Straw and flowers were skilfully woven into their manes before being paraded through the streets where they were judged by a panel of civic dignitaries. During the war years, this lovely tradition ceased, never to restarted, although many of the older carters continued to dress their horses on May Day it was only as a mark of respect, honouring the horses on their birthday.

At 11.30am, as the first horse to be auctioned left its warm hay-green stall to walk down the ramp into the cold, damp day, a ray of watery sunshine momentarily broke through the heavy leaden sky and fancifully I hoped it was a good omen.

There was a goodly crowd assembled to witness the auction. The dealers looking for a bargain, the knacker men, commissioned to supply flesh for the big cats at Bellevue Zoo and a few elderly farmers who clung to the old ways of farming with horses. There were also plenty of old carters who had come to pay their last respects to a way of life never to be seen again.

I was at the sale to purchase as many of the horses as possible on behalf of the Blue Cross Society and, if successful, to find good working homes for them.

The bidding started slowly giving the impression that no one was interested in buying these lovely animals, until eventually an opening bid was made and the whole thing gradually gathered momentum until the bids were coming fast and furious, I was determined to do my damnedest to deliver the magnificent, trusting animals from the clutches of the knackers. I held off my bid until each horse reached £50 then I moved in with my bid. It was a successful tactic and before the short, cloud darkened day had dragged itself towards an early evening I had bought all nine horses for between fifty-seven and a half guineas and ninety guineas each.

The next part of the job, finding homes for the horses, was surprisingly easy. Most went to farmers who, for various reasons, did not want to mechanise. One found a new life as a barge horse on the Bridgewater Canal, and a rather elderly, chubby chap with a moustache like a Sergeant major, too old for any real work came home with me. His name was Major.

It had been sixteen years since Major, the old bay gelding had last seen grass and he was unsure of it, not realising that it was edible. He sniffed and snorted at the sweet young shoots, enjoying the tickling sensation on his moustache and upper lip. He pawed deep furrows in the soft earth with his big iron shod feet and felt his knees and hocks quiver as a long forgotten need to get down and roll overtook him. Major either resisted the desire or had forgotten how it was done and remained upright, perhaps as well because his investigations were interrupted by the arrival of three ponies full of curiosity and cheek. If Major was bewildered by the smallness of the trio, they were no less taken aback by his size, seventeen hands to the wither and full of muscle.

The most daring of the ponies, a pretty, grey Welsh mountain pony named Knucklebone, stretched out his neck in an attempt to reach the big horses nostrils with his own by way of introduction. Major lowered his great head to meet his advances. The pony sniffed at his questioning muzzle, spun around and planted two small sharp hooves on the big horse's chest. Major merely rocked back on his hocks, surprised by this rude behaviour, he was not at all sure how to react, not having socialised for so many years.

The ponies, excited by the presence of the new horse, began to show off. With tails held high, necks arched, blowing hard and noisily, they treated the big gelding to a blatant display of their beauty. All three moved around him in a slow elevated trot only to set off at a headlong gallop up to the top of Rabbit Hill, where they stopped to look back as if to see what impression they had made upon the intruder.

Major took it into his head to follow, but felt unable to move without the word of command from a driver and, besides, the soft conditions under his feet felt decidedly unsafe to him after so many years on the hard, and unyielding city streets. The gang of three were now on their way back at a fearsome pace, bucking and twisting as each tried to out manoeuvre the other. When they came to within a safe distance of the Clydesdale, all three put the breaks on in unison and skidded to a turf-tearing halt before setting off again for the hill. This time Major threw caution to the wind and set off after them in a great shambling trot to begin his short but happy retirement

The retired "Major"

Horses thrive on routine, work and a good diet. Retirement for those that have worked hard for their corn all their life can be as traumatic as for a human and requires special skills from their handler, not least being an observant eye, and a careful watch was kept on the ancient Major .If Major missed city life, he did not let it show. He had plenty to occupy his mind. He would spend hours gazing into the rook-crowded woods by his field or listening to the wheat whispering its ancient secrets to the warm, gentle breeze that stirred its memory.

Until recently, this land had changed very little since the time of the William the bastard and his ragbag army of half-bred Vikings. They indulged in a policy of scorched earth that almost denuded the terrain of usable timber. So little timber was available that to this day many, still occupied, old buildings in the North West are built on a framework of ancient ships timbers, bought when the wooden navy was sold off to make way for more substantial iron, steam ships, powered by coal

The old horse was kept reasonably busy doing jobs around the stables such as harrowing the ménage, carting hay and straw and helping with fencing and any other odd jobs where he could feel that he was earning the corn that was fed to him each evening on his return to the stable, while his companion, a lean black cat, slept on his warm back and dreamed her evil black cat dreams.

During the equine holocaust of the 40s and 50s it was reported in one newspaper that, with luck, the only heavy horses left by the 1960s would be in zoos. Indeed it almost came to that and had it not been for the hard work and dedication of the Shire horse and Clydesdale Societies, these ancient breeds would have become extinct. Heavy horses became a curiosity, those remaining, such as Major, became minor celebrities. He was asked to draw the local rose queen, sat proud on her throne atop an old farm cart, lead carnivals and put in appearances at a few civic events. He visited schools and old folk's clubs, he loved every minute of it, never once disgracing himself. But alas, time; the great robber was beginning to call the big horse and he was enjoying life less and less. Weight had started to drop off him and he lost all interest in working. I couldn't see him suffering like this and so in the autumn, before the bitter, wet, northern winter could add to his misery ,I led him into the yard for the last time. As we passed the old cart

A Reckless Ride

that he had drawn so often, he stopped and then carefully manoeuvred himself backward into position for the shafts to be lowered to his sides. I had not the heart to take him away from the hay wagon, he could not have told me more eloquently that this was where he wanted to end his time and his last request was not denied.

KALIBRE
Chapter 5

The snow scoured hills of Rostov-on-Don, close to the temperamental, shallow, inland Sea of Azov in Mother Russia can be as inhospitable as it is beautiful. The short, butterfly blessed summers produced an abundance of good grazing and in the cultivated southern areas, a hay crop that was rich in herbs and varied, tough grasses on which horses thrive.

In this environment of endless wind, searing, insect-biting heat and wicked blizzards, where four seasons can be experienced in one hour and shelter is almost unheard of, young horses from the State studs would spend their summers playing grown up horse games on gangly young legs, growing strong and agile.

Their time at Rostov was not all pleasant. For it was here in the autumn of the year after the mean-spirited flies had departed and before the cruel, penetrating fingers of Comrade Frost had unfolded, the colts and fillies were rounded up and driven down to the holding pens and barns to be branded and any males considered unfit for breeding, castrated.

The branding and gelding was carried out without the mercy of anaesthetics. Horses were immobilised by twisting a loop of cord around the left ear. This `twitching` of the ear caused many otherwise good horses to become difficult to bridle for the rest of their lives. Another method of restraint used was to grab the skin of a shoulder in both hands and twist as hard as possible.

The horses grew strong and tough. There was no place in the Communist State for weakness or non conformity in man or beast, particularly in the animals that Kalibre herded with, as they were part of a state breeding programme aimed at producing a superior remount for the cavalry and culling was ruthless.

Kalibre was a rich chestnut gelding of the Buddeny breed and a product of the selective breeding programs begun in the 1920s, the foundation mares of which were the strong hardy Don horses crossed with English thoroughbred stallions. The young male offspring's were in turn, put to Don Mares in an endeavour to get even tougher warhorses. Further thoroughbred blood was introduced where it was thought beneficial. The resulting 'breed' was named after the illustrious General Budenny (1883-1975), one time commander of the 1st Cavalry and later, Inspector of Cavalry, a position he held on two occasions.

Before the three and four year old horses were sent out to various cavalry regiments, they were performance-tested for their endurance, jumping and basic dressage ability. Any not up to scratch could face a life of undignified and unimagined hardship on the disastrous collective farms. A few fortunate animals would go to the riding academies where chosen members of the party were allowed to take instruction. In these academies, the standard of riding was such that Russia was able to field Olympic teams in all disciplines. The dressage teams were particularly successful; riding State-bred horses, they rarely came home without the glittering prizes. The majority of rejects were sold as meat on the hoof and exported in appalling conditions in order to obtain much needed foreign currency .A few of the better animals were sold for export as riding horses and among these more fortunate chaps was Kalibre.

It is a long journey through many and varied climates from Russia to the wet hills of northern England but Kalibre and his companions fared well. They were transported, accompanied by grooms, in reasonably well appointed railway carriages with regular feed times and

A Reckless Ride

water aplenty, eventually arriving at Godstone in Kent. It was here in 1970 that I acquired the horse in auction for three hundred and fifty guineas and took him home to Lancashire just as spring was beginning to crawl hesitantly out of the ditches.

Kalibre quickly settled down in his new home and within a short time had a good buddy to show him the ropes and keep him; for some of the time, out of trouble. His new friend was Cascade, a small, coloured pony mare of unknown origins and cunning disposition. She was hardly the ideal choice of companion for the Russian horse for, apart from the difference in size, and temperament, the pony was both an escape artist and a thief. If a bolt was too difficult to open, she would resort to destroying the stable door with her hind feet. If she was tied up, she promptly eat through the rope. Cascade was one of those weird horses that could take off its own rug or saddle without unfastening a single buckle. The dreadful animal would creep around the yard on quiet, unshod tiptoe and release other horses from their stables to join her in illicit midnight feasts in the barn, leaving behind total devastation.

It was not long before Kalibre was invited to join her in these orgies of gluttony

and destruction resulting in him going down with a particularly bad colic after eating his way into a bag of dried sugar beet. It could have been fatal had it not been for the skill and patience of Vet Peter Nutt who stayed with the horse for twelve hours, nursing him through the night until he was out .of danger.

The Cascade troubles were eventually resolved by selling the little monster at Beeston Castle sales in Cheshire. Surprisingly, I felt rather sad to see her go, but Kalibre had enough to think about without being led astray.

At first the Russian horse was very head shy. He would throw up his head, spin around and roll his eyes whenever a bridle was taken into his stable. To tack him up, the bridle had to be dismantled and gently rebuilt around his head avoiding contact with his sensitive ears. Shoeing the horse was even more difficult. He was terrified of smoke and for his first few shoeing sessions, he was blindfolded, later, as his confidence grew, thanks to gentle handling by my brother Jim, Kalibra would stand quietly as long as someone stayed at his head talking or singing to him. Initially the horse was shod cold but it wasn't before Jim was able to make a much more satisfying job by shoeing him hot.

Snow was Kalibre's great love; he would roll in it, eat it, gallop and buck, shove long tracks in it with his nose and push the drifts with his chest. When he was ridden out in snow he fairly danced along, snorting and blowing the tickling flakes from his nose. At these times, he was a joy to ride.

As the spring gave way to summer .Kalibre's schooling began in earnest   I had spent plenty of time hacking him around the moors so he was fit enough to begin his education as a school horse.

When I had first ridden him, I had been appalled at his stiffness and lack of balance. His flanks felt like stone slabs and there was no suppleness at all behind the saddle, this made it impossible for him to use his back legs and come through from behind, at six years old he had the balance of a three-year-old. School riding is very different to the hacking out that he was use to, and Kalibra found it difficult. Unable to work on a straight line he wobbled his way around the school trying to find his balance under my weight. He was very heavy in my left hand and refused to make contact with my right. To make matters worse he was dead to my leg aids on his slab sides. It was back to square one for him.

Working on the lunge rein Kalibre knew enough to go around me on a circle, but his understanding of straightness was non existent; he was bent to the outside of the circle when going left and on the right rein his hind quarters came in to meet me. To add to the problem his mouth was as dry as dust, he neither chewed at the bit nor stretched to make contact with it. It was obvious that the whole horse needed working on. Usually when schooling horses, physical problems arise and appropriate action is taken to exercise, supple and activate the horse through work that will ultimately correct the problem. With Kalibre I felt that he had more of a psychological problem than a physical one. This would be much more difficult to deal with.

The lunge work and twice weekly hacking began to have a relaxing effect on him. On rides out he was lively and animated, enjoying a buck now and then, but alas in the school he switched off totally. I pondered the problem for a few days and came up with an idea. Why

A Reckless Ride

not do a little work in-hand. Without a rider, he could possibly gain some confidence in his own ability.

Beginning with simple things, such as teaching him to move away from a prod of my thumb in his flank. He very quickly realised that if he stepped sideways, the prodding stopped and as he moved away he had to cross his hind legs, causing him to stretch the muscles behind the saddle that had been stiff for so long. At first he moved like a man with lumbago, but I persevered. Of course, the classical golden rule that the horse should be loose in his movements before commencing in- hand work was being broken but I had to do something drastic to make him aware of his back legs and loins. After a few sessions, he was able to move in a walk on a small circle and things began to fall into place.

To encourage Kalibre to salivate, I sprinkled his bit with salt or sometimes a little honey. This worked wonders and he began chewing and reaching down for the bit as he trotted on the lunge. The longer and lower he went the more the three joints in the back legs bent and his back began to swing. Soon he was taking a contact with the bit and moving in good rhythm with an active trot, but most importantly, he was enjoying the work.

It was my intention to hunt this fine Russian horse and as the season approached, I thought it would be a good idea to see if he had any interest in jumping. He had done some exercises over poles, so colours would not come as a surprise to him, or so I thought. During this pole work, he rounded his top line and elevated quite well with his legs going like pistons, he seemed to enjoy the experience. However, when the horse was confronted by anything over eighteen inches he was reduced to a jelly, and refused to move, breaking out in a peculiar, blood bearing sweat, which I understand is common in his breed. Eventually I persuaded him to try small jumps, but it was obvious that his heart was not in it and I bowed out gracefully to ponder his future

Kalibre was eligible for registration at Whetherbys due to his thoroughbred ancestry and, under pressure from a friend who trained in Norfolk, we sent off the horse's papers and he made the journey down to Cromer to let him try his hand at racing.

He trained well and looked a million dollars but as the Daily Express racing correspondent wrote of him "A beautiful looking horse, but looks don't win races", as it turned out he was dead right. However, I got a kick out of seeing his picture in the paper.

The day of his first outing arrived. He was entered in a modest race at Kempton Park where he pranced and preened down to the starting gate. Alas, that was where he stayed, whilst the other horses shot off around the course. All very embarrassing, and expensive. We tried him once more, but he ran a very poor race, finishing seventh in a field of eight. (The horse he beat had pulled up lame) and so it was back to Manchester for my chestnut horse. What to do with him? He wouldn't jump, couldn't race and hated to work in the riding school. He was at his best standing with his pretty head over the stable door smiling at passers-by.

Not long after the horse's ignoble return to my yard, I was enjoying a quiet moment leaning on the paddock fence watching the horses play, when Kalibra was brought to the gate to be turned out. I hadn't seen him in the field before, although he had been turned into the school with two ponies soon after I had bought him. This gave me the opportunity to study the horse's natural way of going and learn something of its temperament - was he timid, aggressive or outgoing? All clues as to how to approach its training. Kalibre had shown an extremely laid-back attitude to life, suggesting that he would require pushing a little.

A cheeky Dartmoor pony mare approached Kalibre. They eye balled each other for a while, blowing and snorting; suddenly the pony squealed like a banshee and struck out with a front foot, narrowly missing the chestnut's forearm. Then as quick as a flash she spun around and let fly with both barrels, catching Kalibre full on his chest. Up he went on his hind legs, flaying the air with his front feet. This caused some alarm in the Dartmoor pony who, deciding that discretion was the better part of valour went off across the field at a rate of knots.

The chestnut gelding went after her, intent on avenging these insults from the mare, who, had by now, burrowed her way into a bunch of horses in the hope of being made invisible. It was then that Kalibre began to show what he was made of. He circled the horses in a beautiful slow elevated trot, blowing like a train. He stopped, walked backwards for about ten steps searching for the pony, then forward in an amazing extended trot, only halting when the little mare was pushed in front of him. Kalibre drew in his head, lowered his hindquarters and soared into a beautiful, elevated trot on the spot, a perfect piaffe. It was only a few steps, but it was there. The whole display lasted only a few seconds, but it was a sight I shall always remember.

From then on Kalibre's schooling began in earnest. I reasoned that, if he could perform on his own with such style, perhaps he could be trained to do it for me. He had become, by now, a very supple horse. It is possible that, initially, I had given him insufficient time to recover from his long, arduous journey from Russia or that his race training had taken all the knots out of him. Whatever the reason, he was now moving like an angel and responding well to his schooling.

It wasn't long before he was ready for his first dressage test and was duly entered in a preliminary class at a small event in the Pennine village of Todmorden. In those faraway days it was customary to start a horse's dressage career at preliminary or novice level and progress along sound logical lines through novice and medium tests and so on. Sadly, nowadays it us not unusual to see horses making their début at a much higher level, a practise, which defeats the object of classical riding and causes much stress to the horses.

High on the hills overlooking the village on a rare, for these parts, warm summer's day, Kalibre rose to the occasion and won by a very comfortable lead. He posed and strutted his stuff, thoroughly enjoying the day and I must admit I did bask in the sunshine of his glory a little as his good looks brought admiring glances.

Kalibre's dressage career was meteoric, eight firsts in a row and competing now at intermediate level. Vainly, I began to expect by right to be placed first, I became a pot-hunter, and I became sloppy, turning up at events with hardly enough time to loosen up my horse or myself before our test, with foreseeable results. We didn't begin to slip down the ladder so much as fall off the roof and I experienced a genuine feeling of shock when, one day in Knutsford, Cheshire, we were not placed at all and my test sheet revealed an abysmal mark with uncomplimentary remarks. Of course I blamed the judge for not knowing her job. I blamed the horse for being so wooden. Poor Alison Eccles, The best head girl ever, had come along to act as groom, also, unfairly, came in for a tongue-lashing. Not being one for taking abuse or an injustice

Tony Dampier

lightly, she got stuck into me telling me a few home truths. I sulked all the way home, perhaps because I knew she was right. After this, things improved and he was soon on the way up again, but financial difficulties were becoming uppermost in my mind. My only way out was to accept an offer for my two best horses, one of which was Kalibre. I was very sorry to see him go; he had taught me so much, not only about equestrian matters, but also about the dangers of vanity.

PADDY
CHAPTER 6

If Paddy was not the ugliest horse in the world he must have come high on the list. In the natural order of life there is usually one shining virtue hidden in even the most miserable man or beast, to find any virtue in Paddy took many months of observation and faith, for Paddy was an enigma. He can only be described as ugly. Every living thing has a right to be ugly, but Paddy abused that right. None of the flowing athletic lines or symmetry one expects in a horse were his. No grace of movement, no proud outlook, his conformation was a series of right angles, supplying strength without suppleness, but perhaps his worst feature was his head. It was huge and so out of proportion to the rest of his body that, had it not been for the blessing of a short muscular neck, set into the shoulders of a nightclub bouncer, I am sure his nose would have dragged along the ground. It was this same short neck, coupled to a perfectly upright shoulder that gave Paddy his peculiar gait. His stride was very choppy with a knee action that had to be seen to be believed and the more the rider pushed him on, in an attempt to lengthen his stride, the higher his knees came. To add to Paddy's anatomical restrictions his hind legs would have been a boon to a kangaroo.

However, in all fairness to the lacklustre beast, he was normal in one respect, his colour. He was a rich bay with black points. Paddy's temperament was, on casual acquaintance, phlegmatic, even sloth like. It was only after taking the trouble to understand him that one realised that inside this fifteen hand tub of lard was a fifteen hand tub of lard with an above average understanding of man's vanities and that his sole mission in life was to teach mankind a little humility. This he did with consistency, if not flair. Many a brave hero was shown the error of his ways when refusing to observe the gospel according to Saint Paddy. In spite of the horse's many disadvantages, his teenage owner Linda, an emotional millionaire who could see nothing but good in Paddy, loved him with a passion. She spent long hours grooming him and even longer hours gazing into his big brown eyes, looking for his soul. It was not time wasted, for a rapport was established between them. I would even venture to suggest that a bonding had occurred that was both touching and frightening because Paddy was certainly the dominant party.

Linda never really settled on a career for her beloved horse. One day he was to be a show jumper, another day a dressage horse and later a hunter, together with earning some of his keep in the riding school as a working livery. Linda worked hard with Paddy throughout that long, first winter and when the first green blush of spring came to the Pennines, she announced that Paddy and she were to compete in the Rochdale Riding Club shows every month. These shows were a source of wonder to Linda. She watched Arabian horses flash by, barely touching the ground, and scruffy, sparse bearded youths carrying boxes and rugs in the wake of prima donas astride immaculately turned out horses. None of this caused the slightest concern in the girl because she knew that, in Paddy, she had the best horse on the show ground.

In the equitation classes, where the rider's ability is judged rather than the looks of the horse, Linda was usually in the final line up. Paddy behaved himself and did all that was asked of him, albeit grudgingly. Linda's ambitions, however, far exceeded her horse's ability and on their arrival at the show ground all her good plans regarding Paddy's programme for the day were disregarded and the horse was entered into as many classes as he was eligible for, including, much to Paddy's disgust, jumping classes,. It must be said however, that in spite of the horse's resentment at being subjected to the indignities of jumping, he never once refused to tackle a fence, no matter

A Reckless Ride

how high or wide. It was the way in which he did it that caused the show committee members to request that Linda confine her horse to less energetic events.

Paddy's technique was to go like a bat out of hell for the first fence and clear it by miles just to give Linda some false confidence no doubt. From then on he proceeded to methodically destroy the rest of the course by storming up to each jump, putting the brakes on and then push with his chest on the poles until the whole structure collapsed, then he would walk through the debris and blast onto the next obstacle, only to repeat the exercise. If a fence was built too strongly, Paddy would attack it with his front legs by placing a huge hoof over a pole and pulling the offending barrier to his progress down. All in all, Paddy was a horse to be reckoned with.

Paddy further enhanced his reputation when he met Demetrius, a Greek student of chiropody at Salford Technical College. (Now University) Each Wednesday afternoon the college riding club members were bussed to my stables for riding tuition. Demetrius had little feeling for animals, other than to treat them as beasts of burden that had to be beaten into submission. Actually he was not unlike Paddy in build being square of body, thick of neck, sporting a very long unruly beard and weighing in at some sixteen stone.

Old Paddy, being a weight carrier, was duly allotted Demetrius for the duration of his lesson. On this particular day, the riders were lined up in the riding school ready to move off long before the Greek gentleman made what I believe was meant to be his grand entrance. Paddy shuffled into the school and gave me a look of utter contempt, which I knew from experience meant trouble. Demetrius, reins in one hand, raised his free hand in salute to his fellow students, most of whom were rather attractive young ladies wearing jodhpurs like second skins. I remember thinking, as Demetrius swayed by, what a fool of a man he was whom Paddy would take great delight in sorting out, and sort him out he did.

The lesson progressed quite well. All the riders worked hard and I was interested enough not to go onto automatic pilot as I was wont to do when teaching the less inspired. Besides, I was quietly trying to impress a particularly attractive young lady whom, in deference to her ability and more so to her beauty, I allowed her to ride one of my best horses, which would be a good opening for a chat up later on.

Towards the end of the lesson, I put up a small jump to allow the better riders the chance of a little fun and to break the monotony of the school for both horse and riders. Demetrius looked upon this as a golden opportunity to show the girls just how macho he was. Now I have always believed that, if you cannot speak well of a person, don't speak at all, so suffice to say that Demetrius was not yet ready for jumping, in fact he was a million light years away. Perhaps I should have explained to him that it would be unwise to attempt to jump, but with a shout and a thrashing of whip on hide, Paddy and his burden shot away from the line of riders and headed for the jump. I died a thousand deaths fearing the worst, for Paddy of course. By now, the whip was beating a tattoo on the unfortunate Paddy's flanks, and as the jump loomed nearer, everyone held their breath, with the exception of Demetrius who roared like a demented camel in an attempt to urge the poor horse forwards. With a tremendous fart Paddy took off, his knees folded up on either side of his head and he made as perfect a jump as his shape would allow. Up, up and over, balancing Mr Macho on his back all the way.

Demetrius survival of the first jump inspired him to greater effort, both vocally and physically. Ignoring my advice to drop the whip and stop the now furious horse who was well into his best flatulent gallop. He went round the school as though it were the wall of death. About five strides from the jump I saw that certain look in Paddy's eye. Demetrius was about to get his comeuppance. The gallant rider, sitting back like a figure in an old sporting print, braced himself for the lift-off. At the very moment of take-off, the old horse stopped dead, Demetrius shot up Paddy's neck; but before he completed the manoeuvre, Paddy soared into the air from a standstill, an achievement that took great power from his hindquarters, and so great was that power, that the fool of a rider almost shot into orbit. Seconds later, he no doubt wished he had because, when he came down, the wicked horse was waiting for him.

The poor chap crashed into the saddle, legs apart, with an eye-watering thud, which caused a sharp intake of breath before he slid to the ground where he laid gasping and writhing. Paddy, in a final act of retribution, placed a big back hoof onto Demetrius long beard, completely immobilising him, much to the delight of the chuckling ladies This all goes to show that macho doesn't prove mucho

Paddy retired in the spring of 1979. He had had a painful winter with rheumatism and some slight back problems and so Linda bravely, decided to give him the summer at grass, and then have him put him down before the winter set in. He must have missed his work, for one day the old horse broke out of his field and joined a lesson that was in progress in the ménage. Just for the fun of it, I left him alone for a while as he took his place at the back of the group of experienced riders. Paddy changed the rein, turned across the school and lined up in halt on the centre line on command. Had he come to tell me he didn't think much of retirement, I wonder? We gave him a chance and the good horse did light work in the school for a further eighteen months.

On a warm summer's day two weeks after the sad sale of my riding school, Paddy died in his field.

WHEELING AND DEALING
CHAPTER 7

One of the more interesting aspects in running a horse business is buying and selling horses. I didn't do this in a big way, but if a horse came my way that wasn't too expensive and I had a client waiting, I would have a crack at it. The experience gained in purchasing 'sows ears' and turning them into 'silk purses' is invaluable to a horseman. There is no substitute for riding all sorts of horses and ponies and getting a tune out of them. They can all teach you something. In addition, there is the fun of it all. It is a sad man who cannot get some pleasure from his work.

The excitement of chancing your arm on a horse that no one else wants, or has the sense not to buy. The thrill of feeling that a horse is responding to your training methods. And the gloom and despair when you are sitting on the ground after being dumped, watching the animal's backside disappear into the sunset (this usually happens on wet, cold evenings when you are far, far from home). It is all part of the fun.

When selling a horse I try to match rider to horse, make a reasonable profit and have a satisfied customer who will tell others where to shop. After all, a horse dealer is only as good as his last sale. Traditionally, very few people trust a horse dealer, assuming wrongly, that they are all as bent as a brothel bedspring. However, a dealer with a good reputation is to be respected and, if treated with respect, will return the compliment a thousand fold, of course, the other side of the coin shows if the vendor is treated like a dishonest fool or the village idiot.

It was early autumn and the horses' coats, like the leaves on the trees, were changing colour as they exchanged their sleek, short summer coats for winter woollies. The staff and I were beavering away, mucking out and sorting the stables out before the day's business began, when a rather splendid fellow drove into my yard.

With a shrewd eye I gave his car the once over as a barometer of his bank account, He slid from behind the wheel, trying to effect that elegant English complacency, but not quite managing it. Oh what a dandy, tall and slim to the point of being emaciated, a shock of blond hair and wearing an exquisitely cut riding jacket and breeches. His boots were obviously bespoke and polished to a mirror finish in a Dylan Thomas 'Bible black'. The brothers Moss had excelled themselves on this one. To complete his image, a delicious, long haired blond girl whose tanned legs went onward and upward forever and was clearly dressed for misbehaving, accompanied the gentleman.

As I was not expecting anyone that morning, I was dressed in my scruffs and no match for this elegant fellow. Mr Smooth raised his leather-covered cane in greeting, or was it to strike me, I wondered.

"Now then my good man" says he 'Have you a well bred skin to suit a hunting gent?'

Now, I'm not a man easily lost for words, in fact I can be positively garrulous on a good day, but this chap had me speechless. What on earth had he been reading? 'Well bred skin' indeed, sounded like Barbara Cartland stuff.

I must have been a little slow in responding for his next words bowled me over.

"Come, come my man, I haven't got all day, call your master"

This in the late eighties, my gawd. Was he trying to impress the lady I wondered? She would have to be retarded to go for a guy like this. "Right matey" I thought, "You have asked for it. I'm going to take you to the cleaners"

I pulled my cap peak to him and became the yokel he obviously wanted.

"Well Sir, is it a jumping 'oss you're wanting?" I grovelled.

"Indeed not" he snapped "I'm looking for a well bred hunter"

"A hunter it is Sir, well let me see now" I paused, scratching the back of my neck, suggesting a slow ticking over of the old grey matter.

"I just might have the very horse you are looking for Sir" I simpered.

"Well bring it out man, and remember, no tricks, I have an eye for a horse"

I am sure I knew which book he had read.

A few days previously, I had bought a string of horses in Holyhead. Actually my elder brother Bill, a keen horseman and later an organiser of the Dubai Horse Show and brother Jim had put the cash up for the

Jimmy Greylegs

horses and I had three days to get the money back to them before their cheque was presented for clearing, I was confident this could be done as I had buyers waiting. The horses were just off the boat from Ireland and full of catarrh, having picked up the infection from the unhygienic conditions on the ship..

Because we had paid a good price for the animals, (£65.00. each), a lot of money in those days, the vendor had thrown in a small, weedy thoroughbred for luck. I had not attempted to sell this animal; he was destined for the auctions where no questions would be asked. Now here I was, presented with the opportunity of a bit of fun and, maybe, a profit to boot.

I called out to Alison, my head girl, who had been watching, intrigued by Mr Super Smooths performance. 'Bring out Fury from number seven please'. Alison twigged instantly and, taking a head collar into stable number seven, soon presented the weedy horse now named 'Fury' for inspection.

It stood before us, as far through as a herring, with both front legs seeming to come from the same hole, more than a little sway backed, its back legs bent like a sickle, and its hocks leant against each other for support. However, the horse did have an aristocratic head with a kind eye, and often it is the eyes that sell a horse.

The swell walked around Fury, hands clasped behind his back, enjoying the ring of his boots on concrete. He hummed and he ha'd then suddenly he folded up and peered at Fury's legs. He ran a gloved hand down the back tendons before straightening up to walk around once more. Turning to me he asked whether the horse was well broken, I resisted the temptation to point out to him that even its knees were broken and instead told him of its fantastic achievements. Suddenly the fine fellow made a grab at the startled horse's jaw in an attempt to look at its teeth. He rattled off a load of recently digested text book facts about tables and centrals, parrot mouths and wolf teeth. Then again without any warning he skipped back to the horses legs 'I think his legs are rather thin' he announced. 'Dearie me Sir' I said, 'you trot him on these hard roads for a few weeks and his legs will soon thicken up'. 'Yes, of course I know that' he replied, looking at me as though I was some sort of idiot.

While all this was going on, Miss Long legs was putting on a wonderful performance to which my eye was constantly straying, striking poses, caressing the flash car in a most unwholesome manor and draping her lush young body around an equally leggy adolescent weeping willow. Paul, my young trainee, was in love with her for the rest of the day, but he was a walking hormone anyway and permanently in love, he just needed someone to hang it on from time to time.

Eventually, after much discussion, this most superior person bought the weedy horse from me at a splendid price and, would you believe, he hunted the animal two days a week for three seasons. He must have known a thing or two that I didn't and he became quite a good customer. Miss Long legs became a regular riding client and friend, but, being a gentleman, I will tell you no more of that.

Of course, before you can sell horses, you have to buy them and that is a completely different ball game, particularly when buying in Ireland. A deal that could take a couple of hours and a cup of tea in England would take a couple of days and a few gallons of Guinness or poteen in Ireland. But as they say over the water, when God made time he made a lot of it.

Back in the early eighties, a friend and I were horse hunting in County Clare. We got hopelessly lost and called into a village pub to ask directions. Naturally, we were courteous enough to buy a drink or two before making our enquiries, the barman, a diminutive fellow with a morbid face, a constantly winking eye and a limp came over to socialise a little. 'Is it the fishing you're here for?' he asked. Not waiting for a reply he went on to tell us that the fishing was grand hereabouts, the only problem being that there was no water. I understood from this that he was referring to the recent drought.

A few hours and a lot of whiskey later we decided that perhaps it would be wise to delayed our journey until the next day and duly booked a room in the pub for the night. Once word was out that two Brits were looking for horses, we were inundated with offers of the best horses in the county. Of course, we promised to see every one of them next day.

The following morning at six thirty, accompanied by evil headaches, we made our escape from the village before the horse sellers got to us. Three hours later, following directions from the locals, we had covered the seven miles to our first port of call, this would have been regarded by the Irish as speeding in those quieter, far off days.

We drove through a pillared gateway and up a rather gloomy driveway overhung with unkempt trees that seemed quite threatening, towards a small manor house that must have once been quite impressive. Now; it had the appearance of a not so grand ruin. Large flakes of plaster were peeling off in big scabs like an old woman's teeth. One of the Prisoner of Zenda balconies was hanging perilously from the crumbling brickwork of the upper floor and a stunted sycamore growing from a chimney stack clung on for its life, I didn't rate its chances much.

Hanging on a chain by the side of a huge, dark oak, studded door was a blackthorn shelagly. Next to that was a hunting horn on a similar chain, apparently to give callers some choice in announcing their arrival. I chose the club and duly beat on the door. Both my companion and I cringed up close to the door in fear of having dislodged part of the roof with our banging.

The noise bounced of the walls and echoed throughout the dismal house. However, not a soul stirred inside, not even the usual dogs, real or imagined, that seemed to infest these old country houses. I banged again, even harder this time, feeling sure that we were about to meet our end under tons of falling masonry.

'Will you f...ing-well stop breaking my f...ing door down and come round the f...ing back to see the f...ing horses'. Startled, we spun round to see who this epitome of eloquence could be. I remember the disappointment that I felt in discovering a very ordinary looking chap staring very intently at us. He turned quickly and walked around towards the back of the house. It was obvious that we were expected to follow and this we did while our guide continued f...ing and blinding to himself.

We passed beneath an archway where, set into the ivy covered wall above, a graceful, ancient clock shamelessly told a lie and obviously had no intention of ever working again. The stable yard was, if anything, older than the house and certainly in better condition. It was built from grey stone, with huge windows letting in the light. Each windowsill supported a carefully tended window box of flowers. Our host grumbled his way across the immaculate cobbled yard and into his office-come tack room.

The smell of leather, saddle soap and beeswax invaded my senses as my eyes wandered enviously around the polished oak panelled room. Saddlery from all ages was set out lovingly on racks. Glistening black harness shone likes a guardsman's boots, while a full set of cavalry furniture complete with shabraqu and sabre, sat in a place of honour beneath a portrait of a young captain of cavalry dated 1850. The sense of history and continuity was strong, all this wonderful equipment was in excellent condition. The room was spellbinding.

Our cursing host disappeared into a small side room, returning almost immediately wearing a bowler hat and a well-worn tweed hacking jacket. As he elegantly pulled on a pair of kid gloves he asked us with great courtesy to accompany him to the stables. Had the bowler magical properties, I wondered, to change this stooped, foul-mouthed fellow into the straight backed, well spoken gentleman we now beheld.

The interior of the stables could have been designed to house the horses of the great Kings of Ireland. They were the epitome of restrained magnificence. The workmanship was of outstanding quality; the barrel vaulted roof, the ventilation openings and the stall boskins were of solid oak. The iron heel posts were topped with a well-polished ball of brass. Above the iron mangers, the walls were set with marble tiles, whilst beneath our feet was a woodblock floor. The foot of each straw bed was finished with a thick plait of straw. I have seldom seen such a beautiful place.

The stalled horses turned their heads and fidgeted in their deep golden, straw beds to get a better look at us. They were in splendid condition, groomed to perfection, with bandaged tails, pulled manes and not a hair out of place. We stopped by each stall to receive the history and character of the occupant, its likes and dislikes, its breeding and achievements, mostly on the hunting field.

Before we reached the end of the stable, a knackered, old, toothless man with a face like a crumbling dry stonewall led out a fully tacked grey gelding. "Jimmy Greylegs" he announced, was that his name or the horse's name I wondered and thrusting the reins into my hand went about his inscrutable business.

The owner lead the way to a paddock where I swung up into the saddle and hacked the 16.2 grey off down the field. Jimmy Greylegs steered well, but had no knowledge at all of the language of the rider's leg. He did, however, have good natural balance and nice paces, his brakes were reliable and he seemed happy enough to work.

"You'll jump him Sir," I was told. I looked around for a jumpable fence. To my right was a hedge of some four foot six inches in height on the take off side with a drop of about twice that which I had no intention of tackling on a strange horse or indeed any horse, I'm not into self harming.

I need not have feared because a jump in the form of a barb wire fence was indicated. No way, I thought, am I going to jump that. The horse's owner obviously thought differently. He took off his old jacket and draped it over the fence and smiled at me, nervously,` I turned Jimmy Greylegs towards the wire hoping that he would listen to my vocal urgings if not my legs.

The horse cantered nicely forward and I tried to get in at least two Hail Mary's before I died. But I didn't die, although if we had gone any higher I would have been able to shake hands with all the blessed saints.

Jimmy made a huge jump, using his head and neck rather much as young horses do, but a good jump none the less. Inspired, or foolish, I turned this grand horse towards the big hedge. Three strides out he gathered himself for the effort. Again he jumped big, giving me a grand view of the county. I made a great fuss of him and hacked him towards the owner whose only comment was "I thought the good horse could jump".

Later he confessed to Jimmy Greylegs never having been sat on before. Ironically, after risking my neck jumping this green horse, the price increased well beyond my pocket's means.

FAVORI MARA
Chapter 8

Winter came both unexpected and uninvited, bullying away the mild autumn weather overnight. Horses turned out in the meadows to take advantage of the late flush of grass shivered with the sudden cold, danced with the intrusive wind and poached up the land by their meadow gate with a frenzy of stamping feet, shouting their discomfort in the direction of the warm stables.

The Lippizan Stallion ` Favori Mara

Tony Dampier

In the stable yard the autumn leaves that yesterday played cheekily around our feet, like kids let out of school, were reduced to a soggy mulch, whilst those that had survived were torn from the branches and waved goodbye as they flew off to who knows where. Weaknesses in roofs became evident, as did blocked drains and warped doors, their bolts in need of realignment yet again. Loose boxes were hurriedly bedded down with deep, golden straw, and rugs, thankfully cleaned and repaired last spring, were brought out. Hay nets were filled and plump barley simmered on the boiler.

Then we had the fun of bringing in twelve hoses and ponies, all wanting to be first, pushing, barging and kicking. Only Sally, an old grey, Arab mare, stood quietly, distancing herself from the rude antics of her younger stable mates. She would be last to come in and on her own terms, Sally would not to be subjected to head collar or rope, a call was all she required and, if anyone attempted to catch her, away she would trot to the furthermost corner of the meadow to wait for a quieter time to come home on her own.

Into this wet chaos, a horse box of indeterminable years rattled and shook to a grinding stop. From within, a harsh scream tore the air, announcing the arrival of my new horse. From the lowered ramp of the horse box leapt a pure bred Lipizzan stallion 'Favori Mara'. He looked about at his new surroundings and let out a fearful shriek just to let the other horses know that a new, tough leader was in town who wouldn't take any crap from any one.

I had seen him advertised for sale in the 'Horse and Hound', by Frank Greenwood whom I had met in Vienna some months previously. Frank and his wife owned a riding school in the middle of Halifax, of all places, and this is where my brother Jim and I went to see the six-year-old stallion.

What an unruly brute he was, he screamed his way into the school, head in the air, hollow backed and with his black tail, screwing like a propeller. We watched him as his rider attempted to show the horse off. He was a fair jockey but he had his hands full with this chap. The horse was a terrorist. Only a foolish, macho need not to lose face made me attempt to go near him let alone ride him. He was an absolute pig to mount, half rearing, turning his head to snap at my

A Reckless Ride

backside and generally behaving like some primeval idiot. Here was a horse so full of hate I could taste it.

Not wishing to antagonise him further I sat quietly listening to his story as he walked around the school on a loose rein, his whole life seemed to have been spent in a rage. To this day, and many hundreds of horses later, I have not encountered a horse with such a vile disposition, yet there was something about him that appealed to me. Apart from his beauty of form he had a pride and elegance of movement that lifted the spirit. To sit on this horse was to become part of him, to be sharing his beauty and pride. Alas to ride him was also to share his anger and pain; such was the power of his aura. What had happened to the unfortunate horse I wondered?

Taking up the reins a little, I urged him into a trot. His initial response to my request was to kick at my right leg with his hind leg. It was not a reluctance to trot that prompted this behaviour, but an objection to my leg daring to squeeze him at all. Eventually he decided to trot, we almost floated around the school. I then asked for a canter, he responded with a series of vicious bucks that all but unseated me. To add to the joys of riding this horse, the animal's steering was non existent and his brakes were in dire need of readjusting. On reflection, I still do not know why I bought him or, once I had bought him, why I persevered with him for so long.

He came out of the horse box like a kite on a piece of string, shouting and screaming to announce his presence and it took quite some nerve to lead him to his new stable. Mara's insecurity was such that he developed a very strong sense of territory in his stable, he would not be groomed, tacked up or even allow a feed to be taken into him. To catch him, a long grappling hook had to be slipped over the nose band of his head collar and twisted. He was then clipped to a short rope secured to the wall. Grooming him in his stable required the agility of a ballet dancer and nerves of steel. Initially I would not allow any other person to handle this horse except myself, as I was not prepared to risk injury to anybody with what was a rather silly self-indulgence on my part.

In all the ten years that Mara and I were together, he never really got over his aversion to being handled in a stable, but when he was tied outside he behaved like a pussy-cat, grooming, shoeing and washing were no problem.

To begin with, I just hacked Mara around the hills and moors of South Lancashire, occasionally popping over one of the ancient dry stone walls that march on forever over the hills. We wandered through forgotten valleys of Ashworth that had once been alive with industry in the days of King Cotton. Through deserted villages crumbling back into the very earth that had given them birth. Nature has reclaimed much of this part of England, yet civilisation has left unexpected memorials in the shape of roses, marigolds, privet and cherry blossom, all evacuees from long forgotten gardens.

My Brother Chris... The Test Pilot

Gradually this unhappy horse began to enjoy his work, especially if he was in the company of other horses, to whom he was very protective, particularly the mares, to these ladies he behaved with great chivalry, though he did chat up the prettiest with low rumbles as he passed by.

It was, I suppose, inevitable that, with his almost pure white coat, long mane and tail and sheer presence, Favori Mara would become something of a minor celebrity amongst the locals. When we stopped at the 'Pack Horse' on Elbut Lane for a drink, he preened and posed for his public and invariably got the desired response of a Polo mint or a bucket of beer slops. After six months of hacking about and trying to get to know him, I decided the time had come to give him some serious schooling. What a joke, the horse had no intention of trotting endlessly around a boring school, kicking up dust into his eyes and nostrils. I insisted, he resisted, after three months, he was still not prepared to give an inch. I decided that the best course of action was to take him back to basics.

As I tacked him up for lunging, I reasoned that if I established some eye contact he just might give me his attention. Big mistake, any eye contact was taken as a challenge and he reacted quickly and violently. Alas, looking into his eyes was like trying the make contact through a confessional grille, without the benefits of absolution. I sent Mara out onto left rein and he bounded forward in a beautifully elevated canter for four or five strides before spinning round to gallop straight at me, ears back, teeth bared and tail spinning. With the stupidity of youth I stood my ground, for about a second, until the evil sod went up onto his back legs and flayed out with his front feet. 'Oh dear' I thought, or worse, as I ducked under the onslaught of iron rimmed feet, 'time to go.

I legged it across the school to the safety of the gallery at a speed I didn't know I possessed, with the horse from hell breathing fire and brimstone down my neck. Once in the relative safety of the viewing galley, Mara stood as close as he could to the barrier that was between us, the lunge rein was wrapped around his neck and legs, with the end still miraculously in my hand. We eye balled each other and I swear he was laughing at me.

Oh, I did try hard to think gracious thoughts, to analyse his behaviour, to think of patience and love and forgiveness, I tried to look upon this horse as an intellectual challenge. After much theorising, I looked him straight in the eye and spoke quietly. Right you bad bastard, if you want to do it the hard way that's how we will play it. I didn`t really know what the hard way was but I`m sure he did.

Leaning over the rail, I clipped side reins to his bit. They were a little short but I didn't let them out, as I wanted the horse to feel some measure of control. In the training area I sent him out again on the left rein, expecting the worst. The contrary animal behaved impeccably, floating along in the rounded trot that is typical of his breed and with a lovely arched top line. The joints of his back legs flexed in an exaggerated way to push and lift his body forward, he was a joy to behold. It was to take many months of work before he went in the same way with me on top.

    I whistled to get his attention and brought the sour horse to a walk, I loved the way he lowered his hindquarters during transitions down from one pace to another. Again, I whistled to him and he came to a halt, a look came into his eye that meant trouble and he made a move towards me. I stared him out, raised once finger to him and growled 'Hey'; the stallion stopped moving and dropped his head to avoid eye contact. Ah, had I made a break through I wondered? Changing quietly to the right rein, Favori Mara showed a very marked hollowness and reluctance to make as much of an effort in his work. This hollowness, however, was not the result of injury or pain; it was quite natural and I would be able to correct it with patience and time.

    From these early morning lunging sessions and hacks, a rapport was beginning to be established, but not in a way that I had expected, for I found myself responding to his body language and his demands rather than he to mine and, because of this, he gradually began to discount me as a threat and relaxed in my company and when I rode him. I also relaxed and began to feed him ideas. I placed him in positions where the easiest thing for him to do was exactly what I wanted him to do.

    In the school, if he went into canter, I let him carry on until I felt he was ready to trot, then I would shift my weight slightly and soften my seat to help him make a decision and a comfortable transition down. In this way, he began to respond to the lightest of aids until all I had to do was turn my shoulders in the direction I wanted him to go and he would oblige.

    After a while, I was able to introduce a very gentle leg pressure at the same time as I moved my shoulders and Mara began to understand the language of the aids. This opened the door to slightly more advanced school movements such as leg yielding which gives the rider a little more control of the horse's hindquarters and the most valuable gymnastic movement of all, shoulder- in, where the horses shoulder is brought in from the track he is working on, whilst the hind legs stay on the track. That is of course an over simplification. This exercise, 'invented' in 1733 by Francois de la Gueriniere has often been a subject of controversy, not in its unquestionable value but in how it should be ridden, Even Gueriniere contradicts himself when writing of the movement in his 'Ecole de Cavalerie' It seems that it took his friend Charles Cavedish, Duke of Newcastle to clarify the situation.

Favori Mara was always a forward going horse who loved to take a light contact on the rein and this made things much easier than they might otherwise have been if I had had to chase him on. Over the years, Mara and I became great friends, although he was still not keen to have me in his stable.

"Favori Mara" the Lappizan Stallion

I have found stallions to be much more giving, bold and companionable than mares or geldings. But a stallion must be respected before he will respect, nor must he be treated as a freak, being locked in the stable twenty three hours out of twenty four, as many are. They need to be able to see plenty going on around them and they should be out, in the company of other horses, grazing, hacking and schooling.

A stallion's natural role in life is to procreate and protect and Mara was no exception. He was turned out with geldings and mares out of season, where he selected a small band of three or four companions to look after and he became a very contented horse. All this helped to improve his disposition and his attitude towards schooling. He began to offer movements which were more advanced such as piaffe, passage and lavade.

The friendship between us was such that Mara and I even went on holiday together, although I must confess that It was partly because he wasn't to be trusted in the care of anyone else had I left him at home. He enjoyed splashing about in the sea, galloping along the beach and exploring new territory. I also took him for a few weeks schooling with Franz Rohcowansky, one time chief rider at the Spanish Riding School in Vienna. Rocky thought we were both quite mad and deserved each other, I am sure he was right.

Meanwhile, on the home front, things were not going well. Financial hardships. forced the sale of my business, it all had to be auctioned off, piece by piece, horse by horse. My dear lovely friends all gone under the hammer, it was heartbreaking.

It was about six months later when I heard that Mara was for sale again. My fortunes had improved a little, to the point where I was able to contemplate having my own horse again and so I arranged to go and see the old fellow.

On arrival at the stables where Mara lived, I was impressed by the cleanliness and the condition of the six horses standing in good loose boxes, well bedded down and with full hay nets. These, I was to discover a few minutes later, were the lucky ones.

A surly looking young female knuckle dragger appeared and I explained why I was there. The only response was a nod before she led the way around the back of the stables in a most peculiar crab like way. into the dirtiest, untidy mess I have ever seen. I could see that it had once been a grand stone built stable yard, but was now sadly falling from grace, with roof tiles falling off and guttering hanging down.

The silent girl motioned with the flick of her head towards a closed shed. I opened the top door and peered into the gloom. The stench of urine was so overpowering that my eyes soon began to water making it difficult to focus into the dark interior of what passed for a stable. Eventually I could make out the shape of a horse on the floor. Favori Mara was lying in a pool of his own excrement, a few strands of straw were in evidence from days ago, and his once white coat was now stained yellow. Muck buttons clung desperately to his bony flanks and his hocks and knees were skinned and bloody where they had dragged across the concrete floor. He was a sad sight, but what really hurt was the total lack of life in his once bright, intelligent eyes. It was clear that the horse was dying.

Hurriedly, I tried to get in touch with Mara's owner at his clothing factory. The man wouldn't speak to me; he knew what I was after. In desperation I left a message with his horrified secretary to the effect that if the horse was not humanely destroyed within the hour, the Police, RSPCA and local press would be called in. This produced results, in due course, the knackers wagon arrived and I slowly led my old friend out into the sunlight for the last time.

Once Mara had gone, I stormed up to the farmhouse, where the man was now hiding. Without bothering to knock I strode in, bloody head collar in my hand. The man saw my anger and burst into tears as I wrapped the head collar around his fleshy neck and threw the miserable wretch into a corner where he lay cowering.

About two weeks later I had a phone call from this wretched person, he asked me to supply him with photographs of Mara so that he could have a portrait painted from them; he loved the horse so much. I will not record my reply.

NOTARIO
CHAPTER 9

Once upon a time, on the island of Cyprus, I managed a beautiful stable of outstanding horses. It was a wonderful place to live and work. A time of balmy, summer evenings when the air was heavy with the exotic smells of oranges and bougainvillea and impromptu barbecues, Of long rides in the hills south of Nicosia, interrupted only to picnic on fruit and cobs of dark bread, covered in slices of haloumi cheese and tomato, with good Cypriot wine to help it down as we watched the horses graze among the twisty-trunked olive trees. I recall the lovely, olive-skinned

An over enthusiastic Notario

Tony Dampier

Notario

girls with eyes like fawns and good friends on warm beaches and the cool, clean air of the Troodos Mountains with their unique spicy fragrance of pine and wood smoke. My wife and two youngest children, Matthew and Rebecca seemed to store up the sunshine in their faces to be used in the short, mild winter.

One of my most treasured memories of my time in Cyprus is of the most superb horse I have ever had the privilege to know. His name was Notario, a light grey, Portuguese, Lusitano stallion with a long, black, mane and tail. He looked like a magical horse from a fairy story, or perhaps the faithful mount of some great Warrior who's shared epic adventures and daring deeds would be woven into poems and sagas around camp-fires on dark nights. His action was extravagant and exciting and he took life at full speed, no doubt, a legacy of his days spent training for the Portuguese bullring where swiftness and accuracy were necessary to his survival among the huge black bulls.

It is said, "Who-so-ever would be a power in the east must first hold Cyprus in the hand". Such was once the strategic importance of the island. This belief has caused Cyprus much grief in the past. Situated only 40 miles south of the Turkish coast, 60 miles west of Syria and 150 miles north of the Nile Delta. Over the years Greece, Rome, Venice, Turkey and Great Britain have occupied Cyprus. Mark Anthony made a gift of the island to Cleopatra and her sister. Richard the

A Reckless Ride

Lion heart took possession of the port of Limassol in an act of revenge on the King of Cyprus for his treatment of his wife to be. More recently, since 1974, Turkey has occupied the northern half of the island.

It takes an extraordinary brave man to sink his all into such an apparently fragile political and economical situation. Such a man was George Paraskevaides OBE.

Fiercely proud of his origins and not afraid to put his money where his mouth is, George built up a powerful business empire based on civil engineering, an empire that was lost to him in 1974 when the Turkish invasion robbed him of his lands and his business. Not being one to sit and grieve George started again and rebuilt his business .Not all his ventures have been for profit either. He has built and maintained hospitals and schools, sponsored young Cypriots to study at the best Universities in the world, and rewarded loyalty in his employees.

One of George Paraskevaides dreams for Cyprus (and horse mad daughters Leone and Christina) came to fruition in 1980 with the opening of his Lapatsa Sports Club and Riding Centre. Situated eight miles south of Nicosia in the village of Tseri, the club was set among sweet smelling citrus plantations and vineyards. What a pleasure it was to ride through the groves, particularly at harvest time when the air was thick with the aroma of oranges and lemons.

Flying change of leg. Notario

When I took on the job of developing the riding centre, my employer suggested that I purchase a special horse with which to give displays to visiting V.I.P.s. Of course, I did not need much persuading and, that very evening, got on the phone to an old friend, Lord Henry

Loch, a man who seemed to know every horse in Europe. Henry suggested that I go down to see him at his stables in Suffolk and it was here that I saw and rode Lusitano horses for the first time, To say that I was impressed would be a huge understatement. Unfortunately, none of these horses were for sale, but Henry, with a twinkle in his eye as ever, winked. 'Leave it with me old man; I'll see what I can do'. Two days later the telephone rang, it was Henry to inform me that he had found the ideal horse for me in Portugal.

To cut a long story short, the horse was purchased and arrived in the U.K where I had neither the time nor the accommodation for a stallion as I was collecting twenty horses and their equipment together to take out to Cyprus. Notario was sent down to my good friend John Lassetter in Goodwood for a few weeks. I have always admired John's way with horses since I had studied with him in Vienna and I thought Notario would appeal to his offbeat sense of humour.

In Cyprus, Notario was a celebrity. Even before he had given one display he had featured on the cover of the 'Cyprus Weekly', in the pages of the Nicosia Hilton Hotel magazine and the Cyprus Airways in-flight magazine.

Anxious to establish a rapport between us I took care of his needs myself, mucking out, grooming and feeding him. I spent as much time with him as my work would allow and we became great friends.

Schooling Notario to slow down to a more dignified rate without losing any of his expression and enthusiasm was not easy. Perhaps the horse couldn't see the point of it all. Each day we hacked out over the hills, asking for very little, just working towards relaxing him and riding on as long a rein as he wanted to take.

In October, when the fire was dying from the days and life was beginning again in the Mediterranean towns and villages, Notario and I, accompanied by a friend who was serving with the British Army at the Episcopi garrison, rode up to a tumble-down, concrete block farm yard in the hope of finding water for our horses. Big iron gates, closed and secured with a lock and chain, yielded readily to Mike's nimble fingers and we led the horses through.

Neither of us expected to find a model farm but nothing prepared us for the dreadful sight that confronted us. Among the squalor

A Reckless Ride

and a dozen or so pigs, stood a thoroughbred mare. Her head was in a pigsty, stealing the slops left over from the pigs feed. It was obvious to both of us that this had once been a beautiful animal of good conformation. Now, alas, every bone in her body was visible under the tight, dehydrated skin. Her hips stuck out like coat hangers and all four fetlocks touched the ground as weakened tendons and ligaments could no longer support them. The poor soul's eyes told the whole sad story. No longer a winner on Nicosia race track; she had been dumped here to die by an ungrateful owner.

Notario, usually one for the ladies refused to go near her as if he knew that the old girl's end was close. From a discreet distance he nickered softly to the mare and hung his head; perhaps out of shame for man's treatment of God's vulnerable creatures.

As we left her she didn't follow our going but stood with her head down; not even bothering to flick away the multitudes of flies that fed from her emaciated body. We rode home silently; each wrapped in our own cocoon of anger and sadness

After putting away our horses, Mike and I went into my office where I pulled open the medical cupboard, found a syringe and filled it with a massive dose of a lethal drug. Mike didn't question my actions and he knew where we were headed as he slipped behind the wheel of the Land Rover and drove by moonlight to that dreadful place, where I slipped the needle into the almost dead mare's neck and emptied the syringe. She fell dead before I could take out the needle. I suppose that in legal terms I had committed a crime but, morally, I know I did the right thing. That night Mike and I downed more than a few beers

To get to know Notario better I began working him in hand and on the long reins. This form of training allows the horse to perform school movements without the hindrance of a rider's weight, thereby gaining confidence in his own ability to execute the exercise, and it gives the trainer the opportunity to study the horse's action, attitude and posture. Notario was one of those trustworthy animals that could be worked on the reins with his tail close to the trainer's chest. Much of this training was done at a walk to help him understand that he could work a little slower. He came on well, His lateral movements were executed without stress or change of tempo. If he was a little over enthusiastic at times, it didn't take much to settle him. Sometimes in the half pass, he would go to the side at the expense of going forwards, but a click of the tongue would suffice to send him on.

Eventually he was ready to work once again in more advanced exercises. If his piaffe was pleasing, his passage was astounding. Notario hovered above the ground with every stride, back rounded, quarters lowered and as light as a feather in the hand. Later, under saddle, I was able to experience some of the most outstanding and joyful riding of my career with this lovable, generous horse. He made me feel as though I really could ride.

In Cyprus I was very fortunate in having Alan Bennett as stable manager. Alan was an exceptionally talented horseman who had grown up in a horse family in Lancashire, where his father, Alan senior, trained driving horses for a living. Young Alan and Brother Joe had had to learn all about mucking out and grooming before they were allowed to drive even the most ordinary old pony and neither had ever ridden on a saddle.

Having originally come out to Cyprus to help on the aircraft with the horses, I approached Alan with the offer of a job. After a quick look at the luxurious stables, the lovely girls, the sun and the swimming pools, he agreed and stayed with me for four years.

Early one June morning, after long reining jasper, a liver chestnut gelding, under the merciless Mediterranean sun, I was close to exhaustion and very dehydrated, when Alan, looking rather worried, made a suggestion. 'Why not long rein Jasper from Notario?' 'How do you mean?' I asked. 'Well Notario's a good horse, well behaved and all, and Jasper knows his job now. Give it a try' then added 'You'll kill yourself running about like that.' He wandered off, muttering something about silly old buggers.

Next day we decided to try it. I mounted my stallion and Alan handed Jasper's long driving reins to me and off we went, first we kept to the tracks around the estate but as my confidence grew we ventured out over the hills. Both horses behaved impeccably.

As Jasper was being trained for the carriage, his work was in walk and trot only. Notario, on the other hand, enjoyed a canter and this he would do behind the long striding gelding as I drove him for miles around the villages and tracks of Cyprus. Obviously, this was the way to do it. I could get the young horses fitter because of the distances

A Reckless Ride

I could cover, and so I adopted mounted long reining as routine once the basics were established in my youngsters

. Sometimes I would turn Notario out in the school to play. If I stood in the school myself he would pretend that he was back in the bullring, rearing and plunging to attract my attention. He would then gallop furiously at me, kicking up the dust with his head lowered to look me in the eye, and then, just before he reached me; he would spin around to avoid my imagined horns, with his head turned inwards and never losing eye contact with me. We played this game for hours, twisting and ducking like a pair of prizefighters

Not long after the Lapatsa Riding Club doors opened to the public, we had an official opening day ceremony. There were to be displays of jumping, musical rides, trick riding and lots of food and wine for the five hundred or so guests, including the President of Cyprus. The finale was to be a display of Haute Ecole given by Notario. The displays were a great success, particularly the musical ride and the long rein quadrille that I had been anticipating with dread after the tangled mess that some of our rehearsals had resulted in. Notario, the show

Alan Bennet Riding Sandu Khan

off, loved his part in the event and knew that he was something of a celebrity. I had never known him so expressive. He was faultless and inspired. An audience gave him the opportunity to show off and he played it for all it was worth and brought the house down.

Five years and many good times later, Notario and I parted company. I returned to the U.K., whilst Notario was to remain in Cyprus. Back home and later, when I was the Remounts Officer at

Jasper and Notario

the Royal Stables in the Sultanate of Oman, I received news of Notario from friends. It was not good news. A succession of instructors followed my departure, none of whom had any interest in my old friend. Apparently they were all into jumping and cross-country riding. Notario gradually lost not only his sparkle, but also his health. He suffered three heart attacks and had navicular disease in both front feet

There was so little interest in the horse that he would be left in his stable for months at a time, other than to be occasionally turned out into the covered school for the night. Little wonder that this once magnificent animal had lost the will to live. I could not help feeling that I had betrayed him.

Ten years later, I returned to Cyprus to once again run the stables at Lapatsa . My old friend Notario did not recognise me of course. It had been a long time. He now looked like a sad old man, sunken down onto his bones and much smaller than I remembered him. He had not a spark of interest in life. I felt I had to do something to help him and so once again, I took him under my wing.

With a little T.L.C. and attention, he began to take an interest in what was going on around him. His wonderful spirit, which had lain dormant for so many years, started to bubble to the surface and he shouted his pleasure to all who would listen. His coat took on a high gloss and his now, white mane, grew longer. There were days when he was too lame to go out, but whenever possible I rode him gently around the estate and out into the foothills of the Troodos Mountains.

Late one Sunday evening in September, after a busy day when due to pressure of work, I had been unable to get Notario out for exercise, I decided to take him into the school for a while. He wasn't really interested, just happy to wander around. It had crossed my mind that he could possibly remember his training from earlier days, but I resisted the temptation to push him. He was enjoying a period of relative soundness and I did not want to cause him any problems.

Years ago, the riding school had been wired up with a PA system and, although it had not been used in ages, all the equipment was still there and in working order. My daughter Rebecca was in the school at the time and asked me if I would like some music on, I nodded to her, having always enjoyed riding to music, and I am sure horses respond to the right sort.

Beethoven's Pastoral began to build up, bathing the school in its evocative sweetness. Notario plodded on, ears twitching, until the last notes faded away into the purple night sky. Then the mood changed, I remember smiling to myself, as Boccherini's Minuet took the place of the Pastoral. This had been Notario's display piece. How many happy hours had we danced together to this grand piece of Baroque music? Perhaps Notario had been remembering too. He suddenly drew his head in, gave a squeal and began to go through his old routine un-

Tony Dampier

aided by me. I sat very still, absolutely mesmerised. He tried canter changes, pirouettes, piaffe and passage. Oh how stiff he was, how sad that he couldn't make his body perform as his mind desired, but how magnificent, how noble that this wonderful old horse remembered and wanted to please his rider. I am not ashamed to admit that I shed a tear that warm evening on the island of love when, once again, thanks to a horse, I was allowed a small glimpse through a window into paradise.

Notario, my much loved Lusitano stallion

XENOPHON
Chapter 10

An unframed picture hangs at the top of my stairs. It is no great work of art, being a rather faded photograph of a stocky bay pony with a half grown out hogged mane. His mahogany coat shines with good health. His head is quite neat, if a little Roman nosed and he stands four – square, on small upright hooves.

It is a poor photograph of Xenephon and although he is a plain looking horse, he is of historical importance, for Xenophon was the last of the Paphos ponies, the native pony of Cyprus.

This little known breed of pony had inhabited the hills and forests of Paphos since before the time of Cleopatra. It survived invasion after invasion by Rome. Turkey, Egypt and the British.

As we bumped along the dusty, sheep track that served as the only road into the hidden village of Omodos where my good friend Dr Michael Petris and I were to attend the annual mule and donkey sale, Michael briefed me on what to expect. To begin with the natives of Omodos spoke in an ancient dialect that few Cypriots could understand. Strangers were not particularly welcome he warned and the 1950s struggle against the British for independence and union with Greece (E.O.K.A.) was still fresh in their minds. Therefore, I resolved to keep my mouth shut rather than invite trouble. Michael being a greatly respected veterinarian was always welcome in the village so I felt reasonably safe under his protection.

As we slowly made our way along the lines of mules and donkeys, Michael kept up a running commentary, for my benefit, outlining the history of mules in Cyprus and the merits or otherwise of individual animals,

Unexpectedly , I heard a pony whinny on the far side of the square. It did not register at first, to me it was an every day bit of background noise but Michael heard it and was curious enough to cease his commentary and hurry over to the pony's enclosure to take a closer look. "I don't believe this," he whispered. "It's a Paphos pony". Of course, I had heard of these ponies but knew little about them. Michael was astounded that such a pony still existed believing that the few remaining had passed into extinction when the island was partitioned following the Turkish invasion of 1974.

We did not need much discussion before deciding to try to buy the little stallion and after much searching, found the owner in one of the numerous coffee shops where men sit sideways on cane chairs and play endless games of Tavoli or Backgammon. Then we had to endure hours of haggling and vast quantities of thick, strong Turkish coffee, (after the Turkish invasion it had been renamed Cyprus coffee.) The price asked for the pony would have bought a small house but eventually we got him for a more reasonable amount of money.

Riding lessons at Lapatsa, Cyprus

A Reckless Ride

The animal's owner had pleaded with us to give him a good price for his animal to avoid him having to send his granny and children to work down the copper mines. Actually, the mines, which had given Cyprus its name, had closed down many years ago but we gave him a fair price.

The origins of the Paphos pony are shrouded in mystery. Where they originated can only be conjecture but their development must surely have been influenced by Arabian, Turkish, Greek, Balkan and British horses. All the invaders of this lovely island brought over their own preferred horses, that in time mingled with the resident animals influencing the development of the Paphos pony. Over the years, the equitable climate of Cyprus and the abundance of forage and water contributed greatly to its development.

By all accounts, the Paphos pony was a versatile little chap. He worked with mules on the land and on the salt flats of Larnaca. He walked for miles in circles turning the heavy wheels that brought water up from the deep wells and drew a variety of vehicles from rigid unsprung farm carts to cabs in the towns and the fine coaches used by the clergy

In 1936, Welsh Cob stallions were imported by the British to cross with selected mares in the hope of increasing the height of the ponies used for police and military work. This experiment was quite successful but as always, a breed will naturally revert to the type of horse most suitable to its environment.

For the first three years of their lives, the young ponies and breeding stock lived free in the forests of Paphos. Each year before Easter time, they were rounded up and driven into dry stonewall compounds for branding and identification. Three year olds were selected to be broken for riding, driving or as pack animals.

The method used to catch the ponies was unique. A pony skin stretched over a drum like structure, produced a roar similar to that of a lion when a violin type bow was drawn across it. This caused the ponies to run for their lives away from the awful sound and into the herder's compounds.

During the important festival of Easter, selected ponies were painted with a red dye or henna; supposedly to represent the blood of Christ, and paraded through the streets behind sacred statues and relics. The ponies were an important part of Cypriot life.

Xenephon was a rather lethargic horse, no doubt, his hard life prior to coming to the Lapatsa stables must have broken his spirit somewhat and he was not into trusting humans. In time he did perk up and his hidden character began to show through.

It was in the year following our acquisition of Xenophon that we heard of a Paphos mare living in Kakapetria deep in the Troodos mountains and a search was organised to find her.

Xenophon, the last of the Paphos Ponies

All of the staff of the Lapatsa sports club was excited at the possibilities of regenerating their native breed of pony albeit from a tiny gene pool.

After a few days, the pony was found, working as a tourist attraction in Troodos. Her name was Monica and she was a far better looking specimen than Xenophon and was for sale at an extortionate price of course. After a couple of rich Cyprus coffees and lots of Keo beer, a deal was struck and the mare came home with me.

From the moment they met, Monica and the little stallion were devoted to each other, however, mating was out of the question, they just did not want to know, perhaps they did not want to spoil a perfect friendship. It was odd really because Xenophon was quite a ladies man, he flirted outrageously with all the mares and Monica was a real little slapper, lifting her tail to even the most ugly of geldings but her love for Xenephon must have transcended the physical, as did his for her.

We tried artificial insemination, to no avail and so; alas, despite our best efforts the once plentiful Paphos pony passed into history.

FOUR IN HAND
CHAPTER II

To make a visit Muscat, The Capital city of the Sultanate of Oman, is like a journey back through time. Palaces of white, blue and gold, hilltop castles, Mosques; with beaten gold domes and minarets, surround the cliffs of the small natural harbour, whilst the ancient, dreaded prison fortress of Jebali Castle appears to frown down disap-

Carriage with the Friezian mares, Royal Stables Oman

provingly over the inhabitants of this small city. In this exquisitely magical place one would not be surprised to see flying carpets and winged horses in the warm air above the city walls, the gates of which are flanked by huge cannons, left behind when the Portuguese occupation ended in the sixteenth century.

This is the mysterious land that gave birth to the legend of the unicorn, now thought to have been the Oryx. This bearded, white desert antelope with long straight horns, was hunted to near extinction before Sultan Qaboos took an interest and reintroduced them into their natural desert habitat where they now thrive. It is from Muscat that Sindbad set sail on his adventures and close by the City is one of the only places on earth where Frankincense is harvested as it slowly drips from cuts in the bark of the trees. Frankincense was once valued at its weight in gold.

My adventure was born out of a fit of drunken bravado in the Officers' mess one November evening in 1990. The drinks were coming fast and strong, as were the tales of daring- do and exaggerated adventures from the British officers of the Sultan's Land Forces, Air force and Navy. These were highly technical people who looked upon me, a mounted cavalry officer, with bewilderment and amusement. Most of them did ride a little, as I understand becomes an officer and a gentleman; and they, quite rightly, I suppose, didn't take me seriously as a soldier. But then, neither did I; you see, I was there by mistake, not realising that when I took on the job of Remounts and Ceremonial Officer at the Royal Stables, I had signed on in the Omani army. However I had no regrets.

By late evening, I was well past it, nor was I on my own. We were all out of our heads and in need of some serious sleep and coffee, when some clown suggested that the following morning we all meet up early and go *Whadi*-bashing. This is not some form of racist violence, but a 'sport' involving four-wheel drive vehicles and dried up riverbeds.

The talk began to get into strange things like prop shafts and diffs, petrol versus diesel and something called double de- clutching, all way above my head and rather boring. Of course, I was asked to join the *Whadi*-bash and, like the fool I am, I accepted the invitation, boasting that I would bring the best four-by-four in the Sultanate.

A Reckless Ride

Standing, or rather swaying, by *Whadi Al Fanja* as the early morning sun came up I watched the four-wheel drive vehicles and their bleary eyed drivers gathered for the day's fun which, I understood, included hiding one's head under the bonnet of a land rover or some such vehicle for half an hour, before eventually declaring that they were ready for the off.

My vehicle was the last to arrive. Its approach was seen merely as a small dust cloud. The cloud grew and heads turned to look across the desert in its direction, wondering what huge contraption was on its way to join us. I did not say anything. From out of the dust sprang four, bay, Arabian stallions with frothing mouths and flying manes. Their foam-flecked coats gleamed like burnished copper under the early morning sun as they thundered across the desert towards us, harnessed to what amounted to a substantial battle wagon. It was a sight to stir the blood.

They drew up beside us in a dramatic self-induced sandstorm. Mohammed, the driver, leapt from the wagon. *'Salem Aliakum'* he called. *'Alaikum Salaam'* I returned the greeting. The usual catechism of greetings and replies that must be got through each day with every individual one meets. Mohammed and his crew were *Bedu-ar-rehhal*, pure Bedouin. Their families had been in this harsh land when the Queen of Sheba ruled and men were moon worshippers and although Mohamed was an educated and well-travelled chap, in his heart and mind he was proudly *Bedou*. It was Mohammed who had taught me the language and the mysteries of Oman.

By now, my fellow *whadi*-bashers were seriously concerned about my sanity, as indeed was I, and when I climbed onto the box and took up the reins, with my trusty friend Mohammed by my side, they were sure that I really was mad.

The restless horses were ready for the off and took some handling. It required no strength to keep them together, just the voice and the gentle play of the reins. That is until Hod-Hod; the nearside lead horse, took a nip at the neck of his sidekick Hamsat. The amiable stallion chose to ignore the excitable fellow until Hod-Hod tried again, this time with more success. A great length of black mane was wrenched from Hamsat's crest and hung like a beard from the wretched Hod-Hod's mouth. We were within a split second of a full scale battle erupting and I had no option but to remind the horses of their manners with the lash of my hickory driving whip, and put them to work in the deep desert sand. I drove a large circle, pushing the two lead horses to go into their collars and not leave all the work to the sweating wheelers, as sand poured from the wheels and the ever-present dust cloud followed us.

By the time my horses had settled, the *whadi*-bashers were reving their engines loudly, impatient to be on the way. The nonsense from Hod-Hod and Hamsat had deprived me of much needed time to plan a route through the riverbed before setting off; I had no choice but to follow, almost blindly, in the tracks of one of the motorised vehicles that were now throwing up dust into the faces of the horses, my crew and myself.

The vehicle I had chosen to follow suddenly disappeared over the edge of the *whadi* bank. Too late I realised just what I was in for and any alcohol still in my body evaporated at that moment of truth. And the truth was I was scared witless.

Hod-Hod and Hamsat leapt over the *whadi* brink out of sight, followed by the wheelers. For a moment Mohammed, my crew and I were all alone sitting in our vehicle on the edge of oblivion, united in fear in one of those instants that feel like a lifetime. The next moment we were plunging downwards and I could see my beloved stallions again as we careered towards the riverbed, brakes full on in the hope of stopping the vehicle hitting the wheel horses. That we made it in one piece was a small miracle and, spurred on in the false knowledge that things could not get much worse than that, we set off after the four by fours at a spanking pace, dodging rocks and great holes that made up this God-awful *whadi*.

Suddenly with a great bang, the four by four I was following blew a front tyre. It veered to the left and hit a house-sized boulder before turning over. The screeching of tearing metal as the wreck slid down the *whadi* was horrible. I was in no position to help, as I was heading for disaster myself, with four, now panic stricken stallions, pulling like trains in the direction of a twelve foot drop which would smash horses, vehicle, my boys and myself to bits, I heaved on the reins, pulling the horses over to the right and up a steep, but comparatively easy slope, out of the *whadi* and into the desert floor.

A Reckless Ride

The going was quite firm here away from the larger dunes and we thundered on, the horses now totally out of control. Mohammed, having opened his tightly closed eyes, became aware of our predicament. He stood up, shouted '*Marsalama* Captain Tony, Bye Bye' and leapt from the battle-wagon into a small, passing sand dune. No doubt someone will dig him out later I thought. I do not know at what point the rest of the crew had abandoned me or been catapulted into the desert, but now I was all alone and the horses took over in earnest, stretching out into a full gallop. The wagon bounced and flew over the gravel and sand and I gave thanks to Allah for not making corners in his desert. How we all remained upright, I will never know.

After about half a mile we hit an oiled, graded road, bulldozed out of the desert. These roads are similar to corrugated iron to look at and worse to drive over. The horses were undeterred and showed no signs of slowing, as they swung left onto the road galloping towards some distant palm trees dancing in the warm air. The gallop became a canter, the canter gave way to a trot and eventually they walked, steaming and frothing, their bright bay coats now dark with sweat and dappled with foam, their flanks heaving after the effort of their crazed gallop.

After a relaxing walk, I stopped the horses to allow them to recover from their ordeal. That was when I realised I hadn't a clue where the hell I was. Standing up, I peered about trying to spot a familiar landmark; even a tree or bush is given

the status of a landmark out here. For miles, all I could see was sand and shimmering mirages of water and trees on the horizon. The thought of being lost in the desert, somewhere behind God's back, with neither food nor water, supplies having been left at the base camp, made me more than a little anxious, it could be days before we were found.

I decided to take a chance on the palm trees ahead, hoping that they were not a mirage. I would continue towards them in the hope of coming across a village or meeting up with a tribe of *Bedouin* who could direct me towards home.

To the west, a dark, purple, threatening cloud bank was forming and a gentle breeze was becoming more determined to be noticed. I prayed that I would not be caught in a sandstorm wearing only a

Tony Dampier

short sleeved shirt and a *shamagh* on my head. The horses would cope well enough but without water to wash the cruel sand from their eyelids and nostrils, once the storm passed, we would have a long wait before the natural cleansing process by tears was completed and we could continue on our journey eastward towards the Gulf. There was little point in hurrying the four tired stallions in the hope of out-running the coming storm, which I estimated to be about one hour away, and so I walked them on quietly with only the song of the hooves, harness, swindle trees and humming wheels to break the desert silence.

Tiredness made me less than vigilant, the reins slackened in my hand and I dozed off. For how long, I do not know, but I was awakened by a sudden down pouring of cold rain that took my breath away. I had obviously misread the dark cloud behind me. It was no sandstorm, but a vision-obscuring deluge, now bouncing off the parched land.

This was the first rain for five years in Oman. In the villages the Omanis would be dancing barefoot in the puddles, holding up their open arms and faces to the life-giving gift of rain. The *whadi's* would fill and, within hours, come alive with fish and frogs that had lain dormant through the long drought years, and the desert would bloom with bright flowers and sparse grasses.

The stallions were as surprised as I was by the cold of the rains. I could hardly see the lead horses, but a wild scream from Hod-Hod told me there was trouble. Hamsat had taken revenge for the earlier insult and savagely sunk his teeth into Hod-Hod's neck, drawing blood. The two horses were struggling to get back to back for a kicking match, but only succeeded in kicking the innocent wheelers. All hell broke loose as the four stallions lost their tempers, kicking and biting with wild, white rimmed eyes. God, this is all I needed. I was knackered, lost, dehydrated, hungry and wet through with four manic stallion's intent on killing each other and me. I will sort the devils out once and for all; I thought and got stuck into them with my voice and whip.

At last, after much sulking and arguing, I got them going forward again and put them into a trot, but still they would not settle constantly threatening each other, particularly the leaders.

I gave Hod-Hod a stinger on his shoulder and called his name to get his attention. His ears flicked back to listen to me, I called to Hamsat, he chose to ignore me, though the backwards twitch of one ear told me that he had heard me. I flicked the lash on his rump. That was a big mistake. The devil shot forward into his collar and began to canter, dragging poor Hod Hod along with him. Oh how he pulled and I began to feel my left arm weakening as it gave up the struggle.

In the wink of an eye, we were off again in a gallop down that vile road. I could do nothing about it, I was helpless and hopeless. The night's boozing and lack of sleep had taken their toll, I knew that I was finished, doomed. I did all the usual things that we cowards do in times of fear starting with lots of `Hail Mary's` and finishing by promising to build a great cathedral if the good Lord in his infinite mercy and wisdom would spare my life. I am sure God knew that I was lying but it was worth a try. I swear the wheelers were by now breathing fire and scorching the backsides of the leaders on our headlong journey to Hell.

The rain stopped as suddenly as it had started and, as visibility improved, I was able to see that the palm trees were indeed solid, not a mirage and were approaching fast. I hoped to God that they were not too tightly packed, that really would be the end. The corrugated road suddenly gave way to deep sand and I was able to take some

The team that ran away

Tony Dampier

control and negotiate my way through the palms. There before me was my salvation, the open sea. Allah had not forsaken me. As we hit the deep sand of the beach, the horses slowed a little, allowing me to gain some steering, if not brakes. I drove like a madman as relief restored my spirit. On down the beach we flew to the waiting Gulf of Oman, where the water advanced, bowed and retreated to welcome us. Without hesitation, the four stallions leapt into the waves, enjoying the sudden cooling, and it was not long before the pressure of the water slowed them to a walk.

Four in hand from the box seat

I continued to send them out to sea for about a quarter of a mile, by which time the swell was over trace high. Slowly I turned them in a wide arch to head back to the shore and the sanctuary of a small fishing village where an old man who appeared to be all silver and parchment, shared his meagre supply of precious water and food with us and after insisting that we rested for a while, directed us home. Why do the poor give and share so much while the wealthy give so little? I wonder who are really the richer.

From the village I was able to drive quietly north, along the beach with the surf lapping gently at the horse's feet. I kept close to the water's edge, just in case the boys started fighting again, However we had no further mishaps or equine tantrums for the ten miles-or-so drive back to the Royal Stables where the worried *Askars* opened the great gates to allow us to pass through.

The horses were in a bit of a sorry state on our return, but there was no permanent damage and we all lived to drive another day.

Mohammed turned up two days later. He never once referred to his desertion in my hour of need, nor did I.

Meagic Minuet
Chapter 12.

When I first met Meagil Minuet she was a flea bitten grey, more freckles than grey I think, but time took care of that, for as she grew older she became more silvery grey, (don't we all?) What impressed me most about this lovely Arabian mare was her gazelle like eyes and her temperament. She was a lady in both manners and deportment and she conducted herself with great dignity, regardless of the sometimes unusual tasks she was asked to perform.

Meagil was born by the side of Ilkley Moor in Yorkshire where she spent the first three years of her life. She was a well-bred mare, being sired by the champion Argos out of the Blue Domino mare Shaylee. In 1980, Meagil was in turn, put in foal to the Arabian stallion Rheingold. However, before she gave birth, Meagil was sold to Sheikh Said Al Kindy and exported to the Sultanate of Oman as a gift to His Majesty Sultan Qaboos, where she produced a filly foal to be named Adiyah.

The Royal Stables of His Majesty Sultan Qaboos of Oman, are the last word in luxury accommodation for horses. Situated north of Muskat, by the coastal town of Seeb, the horses lived in air-conditioned loose boxes. Each horse has its own *syce* who was responsible for the animal's every need.

The Royal Stables are part of the Sultan's land forces and are, in reality, a cavalry regiment (now known as The Royal Cavalry) of some four hundred horses, including troop horses, carriage horses, racehorses and polo ponies. The Sultan also has two troops of circus horses, harness racers and an extensive Arabian horse stud farm at Salalah in the more temperate southern part of the country. It was to the stud farm in Sallalah that Meagil was sent to be cared for during her pregnancy. By all accounts, it was an uncomplicated birth and the foal was quickly on its feet and grew strong and lively.

Once Meagil's foal had been weaned and the cooler, winter months made travelling a lot pleasanter, she was flown north to the Royal Stables at Seeb in a noisy old Hercules aircraft and came for training at the remount depot at the Royal Stables.

She settled in surprisingly quickly and seemed to enjoyed her schooling. After her basic training, she was handed over to a group of Omani riders. These boys were a small elite troop who rode in the traditional way of their country on elaborate gold-embroidered saddles with no stirrups. Bridles and breastplates were adorned with small seashells sown into them and a small, blue amulet was attached to the brass chain noseband as a charm against evil. .The bits were rather harsh, hand wrought curb bits with rough, thin mouthpieces. Covering these evil mouthpieces with tape or fabric was one of the first things I did on my arrival at the Royal Stables. The trainers were delighted when I explained why I had done this for the horses were their lives, and the boys were devoted to them.

The mare was soon at home, enjoying her early morning rides along the beach. She and I shared some wonderful; dream like times as we rode out into the shallow waters of the Gulf of Oman. When the horizon and the shore were hidden by the sea mist it was easy to imagine that we were the only living things on earth. Occasionally a small fishing boat would drift silently by, its night's catch illuminated by a yellow-flamed oil lamp swinging from its obsolete mast. Often we found ourselves in the midst of a shoal of silver sardines. Miguel snorted and pranced as the little fishes churned the water around us and then suddenly vanished. From time to time we were visited by dolphins. They came close up to us for a better look and beckoned us to play, gently butting Miguel and clicking to her. She was not in

Migil Minuit

the least alarmed by the smiling creatures, even when one of the more insistent creatures swam between her legs and tipped us both over into the water, their perpetual good humour seemed to raise both our spirits

During the hot summer months, life at the Royal Stables slowed down dramatically. The working day began at 4 am and was over by 7 am. Exercising the horses was done at a walk, followed by hosing down and feeding. Some horses were hosed down three or four times a day, depending upon how they coped with the heat, although often the water was so warm that it did not make much difference. Meagil drifted through the sleepy summer with no ill effect.

September came and with it the pace of life began to increase. Horses and men had to be got fit, uniforms and saddlery fitted. Inspections, drills and rehearsals were organised, show jumping, dressage and skill at arms competitions started again, as did the racing and polo season. January 1st is traditionally Royal Race Day in Oman and was the big day in the life of the Royal Stables. His Majesty would be present to watch his horses and camels race against those of the Mounted police and other Government offices. In between races the soldiers were given the opportunity to show off their skills with trick riding displays, sword, lance and pistol competitions, a thirty-six horse musical ride, barrel racing and other spectacles. It was during a rehearsal for a new display that Miguel and I had our first fallout.

The Omani troop had, for some years, galloped past the Royal Box standing on their horses' backs and saluting smartly to the Sultan. Now was the time for change and they looked to me for inspiration. I was to wish they hadn't. The boys eventually came up with a wonderful idea. They were going to stand up on two horses; one leg on each animals back. Well, we practised in a walk and it seemed quite easy to stand on the big padded saddles, pushing outwards with slightly bent knees. The outward push caused the Arabian horses to lean in towards each other, the horses soon got used to this unusual way of being ridden, once again accepting the strange, illogical ways of man. The next step was to canter. The horses did well, but not so the boys! They got as far as kneeling on the saddle of the nearside horse, but there they froze unable to make the next move. After each attempt, there was much discussion and argument until a new 'volunteer' was pushed forward to have a try; with the same results.

Once the stock of volunteers had been exhausted, the boys went into a huddle, crouched down in the sand while their horses lay around them in a protective circle. Every now and then glances were thrown in my direction, Oh God! I knew what was coming when they all stood up in unison looking at me. The leader of this little troop was one Nasir bin Safe bin Said and it was he who led Meagil Minuet over to where I was standing with the Sultans racehorse trainer, Pat Buckley ,and handed me her cotton reins. 'Test' he said. He was challenging me to prove it was possible.

This was so unfair, I thought, this daft stunt wasn't even my idea. However, one thing I had learnt in Arabia was that one could not loose face if one wanted to keep the respect of ones friends, fellow workers or, as in this case, a whole cavalry regiment and, as we were not alone during our rehearsals, the stands being full of amused onlookers, I really had no choice but to 'test'. To accompany Meagil in this nonsense, I chose an older mare with some racing experience that had worked with Meagil before and they got on quite well together. Riding Miguel up to the start of a long straight run. In front of the stands I turned them around and began the canter back to the waiting Omani boys. I paused to wonder what the hell I was doing this for at my age, but I needed the job I suppose.

Once I was nervously kneeling up on Meagil's saddle, I rose to a sort of undignified crouch and stepped across with my left leg onto the other mare's back. 'Dead easy'. I began to urge them on into a gallop. Within a few strides, they were flat out, making it much easier to stay on board, their backs seeming to ripple rather than spring up and down as in a canter.

As I shot past the cheering lads I let out a victory whoop, I was as high as a kite. The old man could still show them a thing or two, or so I foolishly thought. The left hand bend in the track was looming, 'simple' I told myself, just bend the left knee and lean towards the rails, 'Oh Yes?' The old mare was a past master on this track and began clinging to the rails well before the bend. Meagil Minuet stayed with her all the way. I leaned into my left as we began the turn, taking my weight on the left leg, dead easy, I thought '. Pride does indeed come before a fall.

The inexperienced Meagil tried to stay with the old mare, but alas, she was unable to negotiate the bend as skilfully as her partner and drifted out to the right away from her, leaving me perched on one leg on a galloping horse. This undignified pose must have lasted all of a millisecond but it felt like a lifetime, before I hit the hard track and buried my head in the sand, saving me from observing the spectacle of the two mares' backsides disappearing into the Arabian dust. As I crawled to my feet and staggered up the track towards the boys I was gradually aware of cheering and clapping from the stands, Pakistanis, Sikhs, Indians, Filipinos and Omanis united in their appreciation of my downfall. I must admit to feeling a complete fool. I looked up and raised my arms indicating that I had survived and had no broken bones. The lads roared as I remounted the old mare on her return and cantered past them with a big daft grin on my face. in a strange way my efforts had elevated me in the estimation of the regiment.

We never did try the two-horse stunt again and I didn't push it.

Antar resting

ANTAR
Chapter 13

Jelahl Khan was worried. So worried that he felt compelled to knock at my door at 2.15 am to tell me of "A colic case Sahib". Its better to be informed of these things than to wake up to a dead horse, I reasoned as I grudgingly pulled on a few clothes and stepped out into the purple stillness of the cricket singing night. With only the stars and Jelahl`s flying, white shirt tails to light the way ahead, I crossed the dark riband of the race track that skirted the stable block and married quarters.Jelahl trotted ahead of me, anxious to get back to his charge, I don't think that the amiable Pakistani ever slept, he took his responsibilities as a veterinary assistant very so seriously and lived in dread of being sent back to Pakistan and his fearsome wife and even worse mother-in-law to whom he dispatched ninety five per cent of his monthly pay.

A group of shifty eyed, stone faced men stood around the stable door of a horse newly arrived from Egypt. From their dress it was obvious that these four were the Egyptians who had travelled into Oman with the two Dancing horses, a present to Sultan Qaboos from the president of Egypt. The other two were ever smiling Omani *syces,* only in attendance because they were on night stable guard duty.

The sick horse, a grey stallion, was obviously very distressed, breathing heavily and sweating freely. From time to time he would look around at his flanks as if trying to tell me where his pain was. Opening the stable door to take a closer look I found to my horror that the unfortunate animals front legs were immobilised by tight, rope hobbles. Cursing under my breath I unbuckled the hobbles and rubbed the callused fetlocks to restore the circulation, aware as I did that the Egyptians were in turn cursing me and periodically spitting on the floor. I couldn't follow all that was said, not being familiar with the dialect or accent, but apparently I was a fool and in danger of my life. I ignored them and got on with relieving the horses discomfort.

The stallion was clearly in need of medication. I looked

Desertt Ride. Oman

around for Jelahl Kahn. He was kneeling on the ground with his forehead on the ground, praying. Was it prayer time or was the good man praying for the recovery of Antar? As the horse was called. I left him to Allah and gave the horse a shot of muscle relaxant.

Wherever a group of people, or indeed animals, are thrown together one will emerge as the leader. Antar had no interest at all in being a leader but he was very much the camp comedian. Of course he was very apprehensive for the first few weeks, believing that every time he came out of his stable he had to perform his dance routine and the Egyptian grooms were keen to demonstrate Antars talents. With bracelets of bells secured around each fetlock and one large bell around his neck. The Egyptians then proceeded to beat the horses legs with with sticks until, with his ears flat back and his tail flagging in anger, he hopped up and down showing the whites of his eyes, obviously he was a very unhappy horse. The white horse and his companion, Ramases, had also been taught to sit on their hind quarters like a dog. This was a trick that was later to back-fired on us.

A Reckless Ride

During the spring of 1989, Antar, in the company of five Arabian mares and two mules undertook a journey across the desert to the twin villages of Al Kamal and Al Wafi. The villages squatted side by side on the edge of the Wahibah sands, east of the empty quarter, the wilderness that covers so much of the Arabian peninsular.

The two villages were typical desert settlements being close to water with the original buildings on the cooler high ground. As these fell out of use, newer dwellings were built lower down the hills, leaving the older ones to crumble back into the ground from whence they had come. Sadly the more recent structures are of ugly concrete blocks with non of the artistry and character of the original buildings. The horse from the Royal Stables were not the only ones to make the journey to Al Kamal and Al Wafi. For days now, horsemen had been making their way to the villages to take part in the greatest gathering of Omani horsemen since the tribal wars of the 1750s. Camps were set up close to the castle walls where the arrival of each group of riders was a cause for celebration and an excuse for feasting on rice, goat meat and dates. The parties or *fuddles* went on through the night and well into the next day

Into this chaos of impromptu horse races, drum beats, dancing, rifle fire and flashing swords Antar and his friends arrived. Being from the Royal Stables and the fierce loyalty that the Omanis have for their Sultan, an admiring crowd soon gathered around the horses. An Omani will never criticise or insult another's animals, rather he will enthuse over its good points, ignoring its defects in a way that will leave no doubt in the owners mind that his horse was less than perfect.

Antars *syce,* Nassir was clearly enjoying the reflected glory surrounding his charge. The lovely horse danced, shook hands and sat down at Nassir`s command. Few of the onlookers had ever seen anything like this before and enthusiastically applauded his every trick. Nasser had diligently studied the way in which the Egyptian grooms had persuaded the horse to perform and had now perfected his own little show. Attar responded to the gentler handling and now seemed to be enjoying his work. He did take advantage of Nassirs tender touch but only in a fun way. The boy and the horse had become close friends, they didn't fall out when Antar emptied buckets of water over Nassir nor when his *shamagh* was snatched from his head. The only time the boy did wonder about his friends feelings towards him was when on one occasion the horse whipped his head round and pulled him off his back by the hem of his long *dish-dash* before going off on a quiet hack without his rider.

The horses present on this grand occasion were an assorted bunch, mostly imports from Kuwait, Saudi Arabia, Egypt and the U.K. With a peppering of odds and ends of a nondescript appearance, plus a few real beauties of obvious good breeding. Antar was the only stallion present. With an arched neck and flared nostrils he pranced and posed among the mares in true macho style, and who could blame him. The legendary preference of the Arab for mares is still in evidence. Stallions were considered too noisy to take on raids and rather unpredictable, as Attar was later to confirm. In the old days some tribes would routinely kill male foals as soon as they were born, the same rule applied to female babies.

At 6 am. The first veterinary inspection of the day took place under the eagle eye of the Royal Stables vet, Dr Chris Hillidge. Particular attention was paid to the condition of the unshod animals feet but little dressing was needed, the hooves were as hard and as strong as the horses were. Of all the horses gathered only those of the Royal Stables were shod, having been used on the roads during ceremonial occasions and watering exercise.

The main event was to be a thirty five kilometre ride across the desert, not a long ride by European standards but many of the competitors had already ridden fifty kilometres or more through the night from surrounding villages. Indeed four horses and riders had set out from the interior village of Adam three days before the event and travelled over one hundred kilometres almost non stop to take part in the ride. After the event they would be ridden the same distance back.

At seven am Antar and the Royal Stables entry rode north out of the village of Al Wafi on a graded,oiled road, before swinging west along the half kilometre wide dried bed of *Wadi Al Batha* and on into the desert that was the traditional tribal lands of the *Wahibah* people. In this vast desert, *barasti* huts made from palm fronds, the temporary homes for the *bedouin* families during the nomadic winter months are scattered haphazardly around wells and small oasis. A little further away are ancient burial mounds carefully watched over by elderly tribe members who act as guardians of their ancestors. Among the dunes and Acacia bushes, *Bedouin* pause in their inscrutable work to watch the horsemen go by. While the hobbled, constantly chewing camels in their makeshift compounds look on, as bored as only camels can be.

By nine thirty the heat of the day had began to build up. Oman is said to be the one of the hottest inhabited places on earth. It is this harsh climate that has helped to forge the Arabian horse into the tough, little animal that he is today the supreme endurance horse.After the first check point Antar and his friends had settled into an easy stride, conserving their energies for the hard ride ahead. The going now became more arduous as the riders and horses reached the larger sand dunes. At this time of the year the desert is alive with flowering bushes and groves of strong, dry Ghaf trees that rely on the morning dew to sustain them. These plants are home to hundreds of exotic insects and birds. Beneath the roots, the Arabian red fox waits out the hot day before his nightly foraging for desert hedgehogs, lizards and snakes.

At the half-way checkpoint a large camp had been set up around an oasis, to allow the horses to rest during the hottest part of the day. Water bowser's and forage trucks were awaiting the arrival of the weary

Antar, the Egyption Dancing Horse

horsemen and their mounts. On reaching the camp, Nassir found a place in the shade of a palm tree for Antar and set to work cooling him down by washing out the horses eyes, nose and dock. He massaged the his saddle patch and then allowed him to roll in the soft sand before, understandably, hobbling the horse's front fetlocks, the desert is an awesome place to try catching a loose horse.

We dined on goat and tender, young camel meat. The meat had been cooking since four am. that morning and was as tender as a woman's heart if somewhat gritty with sand.

At three thirty pm. The second and final leg of the ride commenced. A few horses began to tire as they headed in the direction of the great volcanic mass of *Jabal Jahwari,* its distant blue outline shimmering in the heat. We swung north west towards the oasis of *Al Wafi* turning north to ride,once again, into the arid *Wadi Al Batha.* This time Antar and his group were to follow the stony bed of the river on their way to the house of the *Wali* of *Al Wafi* that marked the finishing line. .

The riders and the horses were astonished at the reception awaiting them. Over five hundred people were gathered in the village square to see them home. War dances accompanied by thundering drums, gunfire from antique rifles and flashing swords sent the triumphant horses plunging and dancing towards the colourfully dressed ladies hiding shyly behind their veils in a roped off *harem* area, only to skip back again away from the pretend screams of the woman.

Antar had seen, and in his opinion, put up with enough. As he lined up in the presentation area, he promptly sat down on his haunches and refused to move. Nassir, partly to save face, but more out of a genuine concern for Antar, behaved as if this was perfectly normal behaviour for a horse with Royal connections. After twenty minutes or so Nassir gave Antar a discreet kick in the ribs, the horse grunted but continued to squat in the sand. Gradually Antars eyes glazed over as he retreated into himself as only an Arabian horse can, to conserve energy and remain cool. Too late the horrified Nassir realized what was happening, Antar was flat out, fast asleep, snoring contentedly. And there he remained for a good half hour before he leaped to his feet, yawned and stretched each back leg out in turn then looked about for a drink. Nassir, unbeknownst to Antar had called for Jelahl Khan and the vet thinking that to his beloved horse was dying.

Troop Drill at the Royal Stables, Oman

Before making the long journey back to Muscat, Antar and his companions were to have a few days rest in *Al Kamil* to the delight of the villagers who took it as a great compliment that the Sultans horses should stay in their village.

Not long after the desert ride, before the unbearable heat of the summer had returned, Antar was, once again, up to mischief. I had taken a troop of riders out for a hard days desert riding. Wanting to get the lads fit again after a lazy summer in time for the winters activities I had devised a series of exercises for them including desert patrols .

We camped under the walls of an ancient Portuguese castle that had once been a slave fattening house prior to them going to the auctions. The horses were safely contained within the castle walls, contentedly munching through piles of alf-alfa and rolling in the sand While the night guards patrolled watchfully and fearfully around the ghostly castle as the sun began to hurry towards night time

Antar was beginning to feel bored and restless, moving from one pile of alf-allfa to another, chasing away any rivals for the sweet tasting grass and at the same time keeping a eye out for an escape route. As the sun rapidly set, in a final flash of gold, Antar made his bid for freedom. He scrambled over a section of the wall that had been blown to rubble by cannon fire long, long ago and before the alarm was raised , the wicked stallion was galloping across the stony, desert floor towards the dunes. Antar knew better than to go over the dunes where the soft sand would slow him down, wisely, he kept to the lanes between the mounds of sand.

Within minutes, horses were saddled, men were booted and we were riding out under a huge desert moon and touchable stars lighting our way through the deep purple night. Once we reached the soft sand between the dunes Antars trail was soon picked up, his hoof prints were clear for the world to see in the moonlight. We rode slowly and quietly to avoid alarming the runaway horse.

We had been riding for about half an hour when one of the *syces* rode up to me whispering *"Sahib"* and pointed to the east. There on the crest of a small dune stood Antar, his white coat now a ghostly grey from the reflected moonlight. He didn't rear or do anything dramatic like a Hollywood movie horse. He just stood there looking at us in his usual arrogant way before sliding down the dune to quietly make his way back to the old fort. We fell in behind him and slowly followed, I knew that if any horse got in front of him he would be across the desert again, and so, holding my breath and praying that nothing would spook him I allowed him to set the pace. Antar returned to the fort with his own mounted escort, like some great Sultan of old, trumpeting his arrival at the top of his voice as he walked through the huge gateway into the castle yard where he was secured for the night inside a hastily erected compound with his own personal guard for what remained of the night.

Baroque Boys and Rubens Ladies
Chapter 14

The white stallion stared into my eyes, weighing me up carefully before making his next move. He snorted and lowered his head, sniffing at my sweat-stained shirt. I did not attempt to touch him; such a thing was obviously by invitation only. This horse was considered almost Royalty throughout the whole of the Iberian peninsular and he expected me to afford him the great respect his position demanded. I

Trying out horses in Spain

had the honour of having been granted an audience with a hero of the Spanish people, for this was Opus, the greatest horse ever to work the Bullrings of Spain and beyond.

When I met Opus he was an old man enjoying his retirement, he was still a feisty chap, full of life and with a sparkle in his eye. Our guide told me how excited the horse became if he caught sight of him in his 'suit of lights.'

I had not seen Opus work other than on film and video and had admired his courage, intelligence and beauty for a long time. Although he was not a Spanish horse being a Lusitano from Portugal, Opus style and flamboyance had endeared him to Bull fighting and Classical riding aficionados the world over. This old horse epitomised all the qualities of the Iberian warhorse.

The stables were at the home of the family Domecq who are famous for producing brave bulls, magnificent horses and of course, sherry. As I was conducted around the stud, I could not help but notice what an elegant and cultured family the Domecqs were. I had taken along an interpreter, not speaking very good Spanish myself but I need not have bothered as our hosts spoke better English than I did.

Before going into the covered school where the young horses were training, we had the chance to see the Vaqueros and their horses working the cattle. These horses and their riders would stay out all day among the bulls in all weathers. Theirs was not the pampered life of the classically trained animals, being considered inferior creatures, though very skilled in their work.

Since 1973, the Domecqs had been the sponsors and driving force behind The Royal Andalusian School of Equestrian Art in Jerez until the Spanish Ministry of Information and Tourism took over. Many of the horses I saw that day had been trained at the school and were so sensitive to the riders signals and body movements that any small imperfections in the riders seat resulted in an unasked for response. An unbalanced rider could send the stallion off in an unexpected direction whilst a stiff, unsympathetic hand could provoke anger in the horse resulting in it stiffening or prancing about in a most unnerving manner. However, if a rider sat quietly and lightly the rewards were as a gift from heaven.

A Reckless Ride

I sat quietly as I rode each horse, trying to listen through my body to all they had to tell me, feeling for the all-important rhythm, without which there is no balance, no impulsion and nothing to build on. These lovely animals had rhythm and impulsion to spare and put it to good use. I seemed to get on reasonably well with most of them except for one comedian who, once I had pressed a wrong button, refused to do anything other than a high stepping Spanish Walk. We must have gone around that small school three times before he decided that he had done enough and came to an abrupt halt. I tried to give the impression that I had asked the horse to do it but I am sure that I didn't fool anyone.

Eleganto, the Andalusion Stallion

All the while, the Spaniards stood silently watching, it was most unnerving. However, as I dismounted from the final horse, I was surprised to find my hand shaken by the onlookers; perhaps they were relieved that I had not completely ruined their precious horses. Sadly and not surprisingly, the purchase price of these horses was far greater than my client was prepared to pay.

From southern Spain, I crossed the border into France to the stables of the lovely Brigit Bonnet. Bridget was one of the most talented and elegant horsewoman I have had the privilege to meet. She was a joy to behold as she showed off her horses in the most advanced movements including piaffe, passage and the ultimate proof of lightness, the lavade. I rode eight of her horses that day and I was delighted to find them all so sensitive to my aids and very light in the hand. One very impressive looking white horse caught my eye as he waited patiently, saddled up and ready in his stable. However, as he stood at only 15.1 hands high I considered him too small for my needs and tried to put him from my mind. Oh but he was a stunner. Eventually I could not resist having a sit on him.

The little horse was dressed in a Spanish saddle with a high pommel and a high back that supported the rider, this gave a feeling of great security; also, the bucket stirrups were exceedingly comfortable to my feet. What this lovely horse lacked in height he more than made up for in his carriage, he felt a much bigger animal than he was. If I

Spanish brood mares

wanted to criticise him at all I would say that he lacked swing in his back at first but after a short canter on a long rein, he loosened up and worked well, clearly enjoying himself. In common with many horses, he had a well-developed sense of humour and had plenty of fun at my expense by pretending that he did not understand what I was asking him, perhaps I was being a little clumsy or too rough, however; he eventually settled down and I had some wonderful moments with him. The more he used his hindquarters the lighter he became. His neck arched from his withers to his poll and his back rounded. I recalled the words of my wise old riding master in Cavalry school, he told his keen young students that, "Where a horse puts its head is its own business". Only by encouraging more articulation of the hind legs can we legitimately influence the head carriage to a more athletically and aesthetically acceptable form", here was the proof of that statement. I would have liked to play with this horse for hours; the only way to do so was to buy him, and so I did.

Although many of Brigit s horses were of Iberian stock, she did have a selection of other breeds that she insisted on showing me. A German bred Trackener with a super top line gave me a nice forward going ride. I could not raise any enthusiasm for a black Hanoverian stallion. Although he was nice to look at, he was bone-idle and didn't seem to have a single brain cell. Perhaps these big continental animals require tougher riders than me, I don't enjoy bullying horses.

Feeling pleased with the way I had ridden most of the horses that day I was quite sorry when I mounted the last of them. Although Brigit knew that I was only interested in buying Spanish horses, she insisted that I try a little Camargue stallion just for the hell of it. The horse had a bad attitude towards his work, he seemed to think it rather silly to ponce about in a school, kicking up dust and trotting sideways etc. He tried every way he could to avoid work but once he had stopped sighing and grumbling, he was very nice to ride and quite talented. Unfortunately, after about twenty minutes he suggested quite eloquently that he had done enough by unexpectedly sending me spinning high in the air, I came down to earth in an undignified heap at the feet of the lovely Bridgit. I suppose one could say that I fell for her. Shortly after, with as much dignity as I could muster and a mouthful of sand, I bid the fair lady goodbye.

On returning to my Hotel that evening, I was surprised to find several people waiting to see me. All either had a horse to sell or had a friend with the best horse in Spain to sell. Even the waiter and the chap that ran the bar were in on it. No doubt hoping for an introduction fee or commission. The following morning I reluctantly went to have a look at some of these wonder animals. I found horses in old sheds, empty houses and garages. In one village, two grand horses lived side by side in an outdoor privy, with little room to move about.

The owners of these dejected animals had the mistaken impression that I would be interested only in horses that could do a Spanish

Walk and piaff, consequently schooling whips were desperately wielded around the animals legs in an attempt to get them to do something dramatic, any confusion on the horses part resulted in the addition of verbal abuse. Sadly, many of them were badly scarred across the nose by the misuse of a serrata, the serrated, metal noseband of the Spanish lunge cavason. I did not linger longer than I had too with these unfortunate animals.

This trip had already taken too long and I still had four brood mares to find. There were plenty of good mares about, all proven breeders but purchasing them proved much harder than I had anticipated, breeders being understandably reluctant to part with good breeding mares. I travelled back into Spain where a friend had set up a few meetings for me in Granada, Mabela and Jerez.

For the most part the mares shown to me were in very good health but lived in poor conditions. The stables were small, with little or no room for the horses to exercise themselves. However, the more serious breeders kept their mares in splendid conditions and in good health, although many were grossly overweight and looked much like the ladies in a Rubens painting. Few of the mares were broken to ride or drive, there sole purpose in life was to produce foals and this they did year after year.

Eventually I was able to find a breeder who; being overstocked, was prepared to let a few mares go. He was a hard man to deal with and I didn't quite trust him. He had the sort of face that should have been helping the Police with their inquiries. At first he tried hard to sell me a few inferior mares, others I turned down because of melanomas under the tail, these are common in grey horses, they do not always cause problems but I was not prepared to take the risk. He offered me bribes and incentives but he could see that I was determined to take the best that my budget allowed.

Once we reached an agreement, I requested photocopies of pedigrees and as a precaution, took photographs of each mare from both sides. I sketched positions of whorls, markings such as white socks, stars, a blaze and any scars they might have acquired, I made a big, elaborate show of this identification business and let the man know that I would come over to Spain to supervise the loading of these pregnant ladies myself. I did not want the wrong mares arriving in the U.K as has happened on occasions, nor did I want the additional expense involved in sending them back, thankfully, my client was well pleased with the horses I had chosen and I received a nice bonus.

In the spring of that wonderful warm year of 2002 one of my students, bought a nice Spanish colt from me named Barquero, He had not been an expensive horses due to his chestnut colour being unacceptable to both the British Association for Purebred Spanish Horses and the Spanish authorities. The reasoning behind this was that chestnut suggested an impure bloodline. This rule was rescinded in 2003.

Barquero was a gem to handle and his new owner loved him to bits and became an ardent admirer of the breed. At the time, I was based at her stables with a Spanish stallion named Heraldo. He was a nice chap, dark brown, a good straight mover and a gentleman with his wives, but bone-idle. I lost pounds in weight trying to inspire him to make a little effort, to no avail. However I did breed a nice colt foal by him out of a thoroughbred mare. I still have the colt and have named him Bandolero. Unlike his dad he's very willing and easy to train. At the same time, I had a white, Andalusian stallion in for schooling, prior to his return to Spain. He was a very striking horse to look at but was very confused and demanded a lot of my time. Feeling that he had been taught advanced movements as tricks before he had understood the basics. I worked him slowly and quietly to help him relax, find a rhythm and to calm his troubled mind. Whenever he did get himself wound up, he would piaffe or passage around the school oblivious to his rider's demands. His poor coordination made cantering, a game of chance. He would change leg every stride and occasionally nearly unseat his rider by spinning around in a series of pirouettes with no warning at all. However, without the pressure to perform, he eventually settled and became a much happier and relaxed horse. Weeks later when he was asked for more advanced movements, he executed them with calmness and rhythm.

By now, my friend was so enamoured of Spanish horses that she decided to go over to Spain and find a schoolmaster on which she might improve her riding.

At Barcelona airport our contact, a most ingratiating little man who bowed and fawned over us to the point of being embarrassing, directed us to his beat up old car. This person was to be our escort, driver and sales agent for the dealers we were to meet. Fair enough, like the rest of us he had a living to make and if he oiled the wheels for us, so much the better but I felt that he was about as trustworthy as a politician.

It was a long drive to our first appointment, during which our driver treated us to a liturgy on the virtues of the animals we were to see while the stench of some particularly foul Turkish cigarettes fogged the interior of the car, I felt quite nauseous by the time we arrived at our destination which was a small, untidy farm, lost somewhere in the hills. Within minutes, we had rejected the weary, bay beast brought out for our approval and were on our way to see what was on offer at the next yard.

The small, scruffy stables were situated on two sides of an equally ill kept manage of deep sand with a row of stalls at one end in which were housed some rather nice but small horses. I did not hold out much hope of us finding the right horse here but you never can tell what will turn up in the most unlikely places.

The first horse that was brought out was a bay stallion. He was rather tall for his breed being nearly seventeen hands, quite pretty to look at but had the worst contracted tendons I have ever seen. Dawn loved riding him but was wise enough not to be tempted to buy him particularly after seeing ex-ray plates of his legs. We tried other horses but in spite of the pressure from the vendor, now looking as avaricious as a banker, we flew home horseless and disappointed, only to be flying back to Spain five days later, to have a look at some horses that had been recommended in Banyoles, Girona.

At Barcelona airport we were met by the world famous Classical guitarist and expert on the Spanish horse, Lisa Hurlong, who was to be our guide and advisor. Lisa seemed to known the blood lines every good horse in Spain. Her introduction to Dr Eseban Bosch Frank was invaluable. He was able to show us about one hundred horses.

A dozen or so horses were kept at his home in Banyoles. Still more were grazing on a mountainside overlooking a most beautiful Lake. However, the bulk of his horses were living as a herd, close to the sea. Each stallion had selected a small bunch of mares to look after and lived a relatively trouble free life. Of course, there were little spats between

A Reckless Ride

One of the Boroque Boys

the boys but nothing to cause alarm. We spent a wonderful afternoon wandering among these lovely horses and their babies.

Among the horses, we had seen at Estebans home had been a black two-year-old colt named Eleganto and although I liked him very much, he was not what we were looking for and so I didn't pay much attention to him and carried on with our search for a schoolmaster. I had the good fortune to ride some grand young horses over the next few days. At one yard, I was impressed by the standard of schooling the horses had received. The trainer, a small girl of about seventeen years old, told me that she had never had a lesson in her life and that all her riding knowledge came from a battered old copy of Podhijsky's 'Complete Training of Horse and Rider' and experience with her own horses. It was a remarkable achievement for her to have produced such lightness and balance in all six of her horses.

Time was running out and we had still not selected a suitable horse. We debated for hours the merits of each of the horses on our list of possibles but were no nearer to making a decision when our time was up. As we were making a farewell visit to Esteban and his family, the black two-year-old colt we had seen earlier, walked into the sand school to drink from an ornate fountain that formed a centrepiece. He was an arrogant chap who looked down his nose at we lesser beings that had not had the good fortune to be born a horse. Esteban shook a plastic stone filled bottle in the colt's direction causing him to shoot off around the school in a breath taking display of his haughty beauty. He fairly danced around that school, showing all his natural ability for the work that was to be expected of him later in his life. Whether it was a bit of fun or a cunning piece of sales strategy on Esteban's part, I don't know, but we did not return home empty handed after all, we took with us the most beautiful and most unsuitable horse we had seen in Spain. However, a few years later Eleganto proved to have been a good buy. He became both a superb riding horse and produced some excellent sons, all with his lovely temperament and action.

A.J.
Chapter 15.

The thin mists of the night were lifting to the sun as it warmed the earth and gave it form , encouraging the deer, the elk and sleepy black bears to wake and join in the excitement of a new spring morning.

We shivered in the cold of the high country and sat quietly on our cow ponies as they skittered about in an attempt to warm themselves after a cold night grazing on the sparse, frost covered grass. There were some five hundred head of cattle to round up during the next few days and considering that out here in Montana each animal requires up to forty acres per year to sustain it, there is a lot of range to be covered and plenty of hard riding over some of the toughest and most unforgiving land that I had ever experienced. Most of this land on the Big Horn and Prior Mountains is Indian reservation land and is leased to the ranchers who still work in the traditional way, on horse back

The Trail Boss split us up into pairs and gave each pair a few square miles of range to clear of cattle and drive them to the branding rendezvous some ten miles away. My sidekick was a good-looking Amish lad named Ruben. Ruben dressed and rode like a genuine kick ass cowboy and spoke with a John Wayne drawl that made my English accent seem oddly out of place. I determined to emulate his accent but it came out more scouse than cowboy. I did however affect a walk like John Wayne but this was not due to any acting ability on my part but pain after eleven hours in the saddle each day.

As the sun rose on my boyhood dream of being a cowboy, (and who has not had such dreams?) I pushed my pony; named A J, towards a bunch of cows who had been eyeing us suspiciously. Ruben cantered off a couple of hundred yards to take the right flank. I waited for him until he was in position before nudging AJ to the left of the cattle and moved them slowly towards a large rock formation where they could be held. I didn't hear Ruben call to me the first time, so intent was I on keeping the cattle together. His second, louder call, got my attention and I looked back. There behind me stood a huge black bear. His sleek coat and well covered ribs told of good food and plenty of it, which was unusual so soon after hibernation when all surplus fat would have been used up.

A J was not in the least bit perturbed by the bears presence and so I presumed that all was well and began rooting about in my saddlebag for a camera. Before I could take a photograph, big bears wife and kids had moved in on us, more inquisitive than threatening I thought but my sensible horse reckoned that being outnumbered, it was time to move on

Apparently, a bear can outrun a horse, climb like a monkey and track better than an Indian. Old A J knew this and moved slowly and quietly away from the bruin family. Not so the cattle, who were now legging it across the range. Fortunately they were heading roughly in the direction that Ruben and I wanted them to go so we let them get on with it. The bears had gone grumbling on their way by the time Ruben rode up, no doubt feeling that their patch of open range was becoming a little too crowded.

By mid morning we had collected a sizeable herd of cattle together. Confident that there were no more critters hiding in the gullies or amongst the sage bushes, we started driving them to the meeting point.

The lead steer was a big blue with a five foot horn span and a mean, red eye, he was a feisty, uncooperative old thing and he would make a break for freedom at every opportunity by leaping into some inaccessible gully, hoping that his ladies would follow him, some did, foolish things, and valuable time would be lost persuading them to climb out again. I began to hate that old bull with a passion and he me, I am sure.

One such escape bid caused me to up my respect for AJ when a brown bull, three cows and two calves ran into a small box canyon through which ran a river, swollen by snow melt. Leaving Rubin and his lovely red roan horse, Tiger Tears, to care for the main herd AJ and I went in pursuit of the absconding cattle. They were not difficult to

A.J. and Me. Montana

follow, I could hear them ahead of us as they crashed through the undergrowth of the densely wooded canyon.

Eventually I caught up with them at the end of the canyon and would have had them boxed in had they not now been on the other side of the river to me. Old A J didn't hesitate, He knew that his job was to bring the cattle home and with this in mind, with no prompting from me, he plunged into the fast flowing, icy river, I had no option but to go with him, hanging on to the saddle horn as he stumbled over submerged rocks and leaned into the strong current close to where the river roared from the canyon wall in a great, muddy brown arch

Much to my surprise we made it to the other side alive and scrambled up the steep, slippery side feeling that at any moment A J would go over backwards or slide back down into the ice cold river, but we managed to get up onto the floor of the canyon and continue on our mission to bring home the cattle who were staring at us as they chewed contentedly on the sweet riverside grass.

A J quietly worked his way towards them and nudged them into a leisurely stroll towards the mouth of the canyon. So far I had not been at all involved the proceedings, the horse knew what he was doing and I left him to it yet again. It doesn't do to interfere with these knowledgeable ponies when they are working; just to pick up a contact with the reins is to invite a lot of trouble. Few of them will tolerate being controlled by the bit, they understand neck reining and how to do their job and that is it.

The brown bull took the lead and for about quarter of a mile, all went well, until he led the cattle through some rough, almost impenetrable bush.

The horse stayed level with them but made no effort to follow into the flesh tearing growth. How the cattle made their way through it I don't know.

The brave horse did his best to stay close to the cattle but it was a torturous trail they had blazed, over fallen trees, low branches and cruel thorn bushes. He also had to contend with a rider that spent most of his time hanging around the poor animal's neck or rolling about ducking branches. Eventually the growth got so thick that I had to dismount and let A J pick his way through whilst I hung on to his tail and followed.

We had not gone far when A J came to a dead stop and looked round at me as if to ask what next. It was good of him to involve me at last. A young aspen tree had fallen across our path. What was I to do? Should we retrace our steps, cross the river and run the risk of loosing the cattle, or should I try

Cowponies. Montana

to move the tree; it wasn't very big but it was in an awkward position. I dreaded the prospect of fording that damd freezing river again, so I was left with no option but to try to move the Aspen.

Fortunately, the tree had fallen across a big rock leaving just enough space for me to get my back under and by straightening my legs, lift it. Slowly the small but heavy tree began to rise; with luck, I should be able to carry it forward until it slid off the rock and we could step over it. Meanwhile A.J. had taken the opportunity to grab a mouthful of grass before following me. It was then that he performed an amazing feat. The good horse dropped to his knees and began to crawl underneath the tree trunk that I was trying so hard to shift. Once his front end was safely on the far side, he lowered his hindquarters, folded up his back legs and scrambled through the gap where he stood waiting for me. He gave me a knowing look and I swear that horse smiled at me; but horses don't do that, do they?

Eventually we rejoined Ruben and the herd. Ruben just nodded when I appeared driving the escapees before me, John Wayne would never pay a compliment so why should Ruben. We made the rendezvous on time and after a bite at a battered old sandwich and a swig of water, we got on with the roping, branding and doctoring the cattle.

A J was a great cutting horse who, in common with most cow ponies, had learned his trade on the job. He had never been groomed or shod and did not have a clue about that great English equestrian must have, the Polo mint. What a grand little worker he was. He could not have been more than 15 hands high but would carry his heavy western saddle and a twelve stone rider with ease for ten to fourteen hours a day. When he was working the cattle, one could be forgiven for thinking that he was crossed with a border collie, he was so totally focused. Once he had been shown which calf to take, he dropped his head until his eyes were level with those of the animal and never lost contact until he had driven it out of the herd where it could be roped, tied, branded and castrated. I never once saw anaesthetics used during these painful operations.

Apart from one small mishap, the branding went well, everyone knew what they were doing and worked as a team, though few words were spoken. The less experienced acted as out riders holding the herd together. Meanwhile the wranglers introduced excitable young horses to their trade. It was surprising how quickly these half-wild, unbroken ponies settled into their new role.

It was one of these ponies, a nice grey named Timber, which caused a bit of stir when his wrangler roped a tornado of a calf. The calf was not going to submit to the indignity of it all without a fight, He galloped around in a wide circle on the end of the rope, now secured to the horn of Timbers saddle, barging into cows and ponies and generally causing mayhem. Timber turned to follow him but not fast enough, the tight, hard-waxed rope closed around his legs and he panicked. In an attempt to escape the rope, the terrified pony reared high on his back legs and came crashing over backwards. Fortunately, his rider rolled clear, avoiding being crushed. Timber bolted into the herd of cattle; dragging the calf with him until the rope worked loose from the saddle horn and freed it. The cows; already nervous from the branding, began milling around, pushing and butting each other out of the way as they all tried to gain the safety of the centre of the herd, The cowboys rode to the outside of the herd in an attempt to hold them together. Too late, a bunch of terrified beasts broke from the main bunch and headed for freedom. It only took seconds before the entire herd was stampeding down the valley The cow ponies were onto them in a shot without any command from the riders. It took about two miles of scary riding to head them off and turn them back to the branding camp.

.That evening, tired and hungry after our work we lolled around the big camp-fire telling tall tales of good horses and lost loves while devouring huge steaks with the inevitable beans and coffee. After much persuasion by the trail boss, an aged, Crow Indian told us a story that I will never forget. His weather beaten face showed no emotion in the telling of the tale but his beautiful dark brown eyes would flash with pride and soften with sorrow as he recalled the extraordinary events told to him when he was a child on the barren reservation in the Big Horn Mountains that cover much of mid north Wyoming.

He began by telling us of the battle of 'Greasy Grass' in June 1876 where Yellow Hair Custer met his end. It was a revelation to hear of the famous battle of The Little Big Horn from the Native Americans point of view, it was not as the history books tell us by a long way,

Now in his stride the old man began to tell the story that was to prey on my mind for a long time. It was a tale from the tribal history of the Crow people. The old man spoke as if chanting a prayer.

"The raiding party was tired and dispirited. Horses and riders heads drooped, each turned in on their own thoughts. It had been a hard, punishing and unsuccessful raid that had lasted too long with many losses of ponies and warriors, each would be greatly missed. Had the buffalo still been plentiful the raid on another tribes food supply would not have been necessary, but the white man had decimated the great herds for hides and sport and to demoralise the Indian Nations. The young brave who was the leader of the party reined in his white horse and shouted, pointing down to where a large scattering of tepees, colourful under the late afternoon sun, stood close to the banks of the Yellowstone River. Anxious to be home, they delayed only long enough to don their best garments and war paint.

Heads now held high the warriors rode down towards the great river and home. Half a mile from the camp, the young men halted their ponies sensing that all was not well. A strange quiet was about the camp. No woman came out to greet them, no children ran shouting and whooping, only a loan, brindle dog, tail between its legs, bellied towards them through the dust and sage bushes.

The braves, worried, sniffed the air. And found it heavy with the smell of death.

Bewildered and alarmed the braves followed the white horse and its rider into the village of teepees. Smallpox had felled sixty per cent of the Indian nations and now it had visited the small tribe and few remained alive to care for the dying and await their turn to die.

The young rider of the white horse dismounted to run to the tepee of the girl he was to marry. Too late, he took her in his arms. She had tried to wait for him but her young body was racked by the white man's disease and she had died a sad death.

They built many death platforms and sang to the sky, the earth and the spirits of their ancestors, before calling a council to discussed ways of appeasing the gods and halt the extinction of the tribe. The meeting went on into the night and as the morning sun came searching for them, the youth fetched his white horse and drew a blindfold over its eyes securing it under the bridle cheeks. Leaping onto the back of the restless animal, he announced his intention to sacrifice himself to the gods in an attempt to save what he could of the tribe. Other young men joined him and together, singing their death songs they galloped the blinded horses towards the edge of the rim rocks and leapt into the void".

To this day, the Native Americans know Sacrifice Rock, overlooking the Montana city of Billings, as `The place where the white horse jumped.` Close by; appropriately, is Boot Hill, where disrespectful gophers climb out of the graves of long dead cowboys and mountain men to peep at strangers.

The tribes eventually dispersed when in the early 1900s the American Government not only took away their right to own ponies but also slaughtered thousands of healthy animals. Of course, this was no new thing. In 1858, Colonel George Wright ordered his troops to kill 800 captured Native American horses on the Spokane River, although it was a crime on the frontier at that time to kill a horse, Wright justified his actions as" a means of demoralizing the tribes". Today a monument marks the site that is forever known as Horse Slaughter Camp.

After a cold night in a sleeping bag with a saddle for a pillow, we awoke to a grey, wet morning. The white browed cowboys, looked less glamorous than yesterday; having slept fully clothed and now wearing long yellow or brown waterproof slickers, congregated around an old pick up truck that acted as a chuck wagon. We rushed down a breakfast of eggs and of course, beans, washed down with vile, gritty coffee as we stamped around trying to get stiff joints working again.

It was time to move the cattle to the summer pastures. They were as reluctant to start the days march as were the riders and just lay there on the wet grass, chewing their cud. Eventually the trail boss got the big blue leader moving in a leisurely, bellowing stroll and we lesser mortals got the rest of the herd on to their feet and persuaded them to follow the big guy. When at mid morning the sun eventually broke through, steaming cattle, horses and men, got into their stride and the pace picked up.

A Reckless Ride

A cattle drive is a noisy affair with cows bellowing to lost calves, cowboys whooping encouragement and cursing the animals that tried to escape into the scrub. The horses knew before we did when a cow was about to break away and were on its tail without being asked.

Cowboy work is one of the hardest, dirtiest job in the world. Why anyone wants to do it in this comfortable, technological modern world is a mystery. Yet year after year when the screaming Montana winds that drive men mad begin to die down and the rivers sparkle with melting ice and life awakens on the open range. Cowboys will gather, leaving their seasonal jobs and join the few men that had been kept on at the ranch for the winter work. There is Bill, an ex New York cop. My friend Ruben, the Amish farrier. Paddy Ward from Liverpool, a good cowboy and good mate. And Jim, who, in winter tended his ladies hairdressing business in Pennsylvania, to name but a few. All ready to round up the ponies that have survived the winter and the mountain lions. Some of the mares will be pregnant to the wild horse stallions that range the Prior Mountains. The boys will ride into the freedom of the high country where the castles and cathedrals built by nature shelter the cattle and newborn calves.

The powerful aroma of the sagebrush, the smell of the cattle, the freedom of the open range and a good horse beneath you are the things that keep these tough men returning repeatedly to the hard life of a cowboy.

John 'Rocking boots' Forest with one of his Welsh ponies

ROSIE AND ROCKING BOOTS
CHAPTER 16

The land lay resting under a protective blanket of snow, awaiting the timeless call of spring when once again, it would burst into glorious life, but for the wild life that lived out on the moor, it was a time of hardship and a constant battle to survive.

The ice covered ponies huddled together, their summertime grievances forgotten in their need to survive. There was little else to protect them from the biting wind on this desolate moorland. The occasional gully or knoll offered some small respite and there was some shelter on the drift free side of the stonewalls that seem to march on forever across the north of England. But it was their long, shaggy coats and closeness of companions that served them best as they stood patiently waiting.

This winter had been particularly hard. Watering holes had frozen solid and the ground was too hard to paw through for roots. Reserves of fat were being used up rapidly and it was improbable that many of the little band of nine ponies would survive much longer. The boss mare; a woolly fell pony, knew that food had to be found soon or the lively foal that kicked in her belly would perish. This was to be her sixth foal born on the moorland farm indeed three of the little band were her daughters and in foal themselves.

Evening drew near and the clear, cloudless sky turned a fierce, wounded red that reflected on the frozen snow heralding another bitter night. A sharply focused moon rose, showing its hard, smiling face to the shivering world below. Far away a vixen yelped sharply and a big, lean dog fox passed close by the ponies, as he made his way down to a nearby village to scavenge for food in the dust bins, much easier picking than raiding a farm. He licked his lips, gnashed his chops and gave the ponies the evil eye just to wind them up but they ignored his nonsense.

The old mare raised her head and pricked her ears at a familiar sound. She was the first to hear it though the other ponies were not slow to pick up on it as the sound became louder and the bright lights of a tractor burst into view on the edge of their world. The younger ponies whinnied in alarm and dragged their feet from the frozen ground. The mare quietly nickered to them but they would not be comforted and milled around each other, churning the snow into a grey mush.

The tractor, with a trailer loaded with hay bales, drew up beside the dry stonewall where the little herd were sheltering. A dark figure threw six bales of hay to the ground and cut the binder twine before driving off to find another bunch of hungry animals.

In the moonlight, the ponies, led by the old mare, made their way slowly and cautiously towards the hay, the only sound now was from the crunching of the ice as each step broke through the frozen crust and they sank down to their knees in the snow.

The smell of the hay was good but the taste was better and before long, the animals began to feel energy returning to their bodies. After feeding, three of the younger ponies lay down contentedly in the comfortable, warm bed of hay.

And so the long, hard winter passed and unexpectedly spring arrived a month early, only to withdraw again after a few days confusing plants, birds and the ponies alike, such are the vagaries of the British weather. At last spring came for real, creeping shyly from under the drystone walls and shaded places, driving away the ice and snow until a blush of green covered the land and with the spring came the man.

He moved slowly and stiffly as old people do as he slipped a head collar onto the old mare and carefully made his shambling way down an ancient track way, towing the black mare behind him. The younger ponies followed out of habit, trusting her not to lead them into danger. Eventually they reached a big, warm barn, deeply bedded with straw. It was here in the comfort of the barn that the mares were to foal.

First down was the boss mare. She quietly gave birth to a strong, black colt foal. Within a week, all the mares had fearfully given birth and if a little apprehensive at first, had settled into motherhood. The foals bonded with their dams and each other and soon became a band of hooligans, charging about the barn and tormenting the mares until, one morning, the man came again.

Leaning on his stick , worn smooth by the hands of his ancestors, he studied the animals for a long time before throwing wide the barn doors and chasing the ponies out into a warm spring day to spend an hour or so grazing and playing in a small south facing meadow. Their time out would be limited by the threat of laminitis, an extremely painful condition of the sensitive part of the animals hoof, brought on by among other things, spring grass but the grass also helped the mares to produce more milk for the foals

The mares and foals faired well under the watchful eye of the dishevelled man, indeed the ponies looked better cared for than the man did as he stood there bent and work worn in his old army great coat tied together with binder twine and an ancient trilby that had been his fathers before him.

The ponies were treated for parasites and inoculated against flu and tetanus, their feet were trimmed, and the old mare had her sharp teeth rasped to help her eat without bruising her mouth.

Throughout the summer the foals grew big and strong and at six months old it was time for them to be weaned. The little ones were by now quite independent and accustomed to eating hard feed and grass. Weaning time was both emotionally painful and something of a relief to the mares. They were all safely in foal again and getting fed up with the increasingly boisterous behaviour of the naughty foals.

The little ones shouted and complained for a few days; alone in the big barn, but soon settled.

The old man was in a quandary. He had to sell some of his stock, after all they were a cash crop and he had to make a profit or the farm would be finished. Times were hard and getting harder. Hill farming was tough enough as it was. The prices farmers were getting for produce barely covered costs thanks to the super markets demands for cheap food, the threat of even cheaper foreign imports and the devastating effects of the Foot and Mouth outbreak of the year before.

For years, the old man had longed to breed a champion fell pony and the little colt born to his eldest mare that year was by far the best he had ever seen. The question was; should he sell the colt and secure his farm for another year or should he sell all the other ponies and keep the colt and its dam, she was too good a friend to part with, she owed him nothing; having more than paid her way with the foals she had given him over the years.

He procrastinated and worried for days before making a decision only to realize that he had really made his mind up weeks before. All but the old mare and her colt were to go up to Penrith for the Fell Pony Society auction sale in early October.

It was a good sale thanks to buyers from America and Australia. In recent years, a virus outbreak among the breed had resulted in few foals reaching six weeks old. This helped to push up the price of those available and the old man was well pleased with the return on his investment

A daughter of the old mare was knocked down to a dealer from the Rossendale Valley; (the ancient Norse name translates rather romantically as The Valley of Horses) in Lancashire and it was from here that my good buddy, John 'Rocking Boots' Forest bought the pony and gave her the unoriginal name of Rosie.

Rocking Boots is a lovely man; always smiling through his pipe-stained beard that he claims is home to a myriad of wild life. He has the girth of a good hunter and looks like a toy town train driver, indeed when Bootsy is not with his horses, goats, donkey and Shetland pony he is a train driver, and a very contented one at that.

He earned the name Rocking Boots by being the last kid in Bury to wear clogs, the clogs were said to be very good for the feet and in icy conditions, his iron-rimmed footwear ensured that he was always the first to arrive at school.

The pony now named Rosie; was, in common with most of her breed, ready to turn her hoof to any task. She rode like a much bigger

A Reckless Ride

horse, schooled with enthusiasm and took to drawing a flat top cart like she was born to it, until

One misty, snow filled evening in the week before Christmas, Bootsy and I drove down to Edgworth village on the beautiful West Lancashire moors. Our intention was to call on my sister Jacqueline who lived in the village and take her children, Jessica and Tom, for a ride in the cheerfully decorated cart.

The pony behaved splendidly as we bowled along Plantation Road and through the village where we decided to call a halt at the Rose and Crown for a quick brandy; just the one to warm us up a little before picking up the kids. It was not to be our best idea. One drink led to another and well; we couldn't walk out without having another drink with a couple of buddies, just to wish them a Happy Christmas you understand. We knew Rosie would be OK tethered as she was to a twenty five pound weight that was kept on the flat top for such occasions as this, she also had a water proof loin sheet thrown over her, yes she would be fine.

How time flies. We left the pub a few hours later and a little weaker in the head and began walking the moorland road to Tottington guided by the occasional street light.

The combination of cold and exercise cleared our heads a little but it was not until Bootsy stopped to have a pee that he remembered his beloved Rosie. He stopped mid flow, looked at me; just said 'Rosie', and set off at a trot back towards the pub, which indicated how upset he was because Bootsy does not do physical.

By the time we got back, he was puffing like one of his old trains and stone cold sober. Alas, Rosie had gone.

We searched for the pony well into the night but found neither tracks nor trail, the fast falling snow had done a good job of hiding her. Of course the first placed we looked was her stable yard but to no avail. We phoned the police, the R.S.P.C.A. the local animal sanctuary and anyone else we could think of who may be remotely interested in the whereabouts of a missing pony and cart, no one could help.

Thankfully, the snow stopped for a while and a strong wind got up blowing away the dark clouds and improving visibility. Bootsy climbed up onto a rock outcrop to get a better view over the moor. He stood there with the wind whipping the tails of his long drovers coat as he roared like a mad prophet in the wilderness, However, his efforts drew no response.

At eleven pm, the snow returned with a vengeance and we decided to call off our search until the morning.

The call from the police came at about seven thirty the next morning. It seemed that a black pony was causing problems in a small shopping precinct some miles away. Bootsy and I shot off in his trusty old car and sure enough, there was Rosie grazing quietly in a rather smart greengrocery shop. She was a little miffed that her cart prevented her from progressing deeper into the shop where she was sure the apples were stored.

The portly shopkeeper could not get out of his shop and Rosie could not get in. The greengrocer shouted, cursed and threatened Bootsy with legal action Bootsy quietly puffed on his pipe and said "Ay lad, whatever" quite at peace with himself now that he had found Rosie. A crowd had gathered by now to watch the drama unfold, all experts of course, and full of unwanted advice.

The greengrocer shouted at Rosie and waved his arms, his apron and a broom at her. Rosie was unimpressed and just kept right on eating her way through the vegetables until, to add insult to injury and theft, the rich food took effect and she gave an enormous fart, raised her tail and blasted a seemingly endless stream of direa all over the shop doorway causing the poor man to turn a dangerous colour of purple. He retaliated with a bombardment of Granny Smiths and Cyprus potatoes as the shop began to fill with the strong aroma of Rosies little accident.

Bootsy climbed over the cart and Rosie and grabbing her bridle pushed hard in an attempt to get her to back up. The pony tried ever so hard to obey. She sat down heavily in the breeching strap that passed around her hind quarters and strained to push the cart back but the slippery, wet floor tiles gave her little purchase and the cart stayed wedged tight in the shop doorway. Advice from the crowd was coming thick and fast now.

Suddenly, a skinny little girl of about thirteen years dressed in her school uniform, leapt up on to the back of the cart and in a flash, was astride Rosie's back. Taking up the reins, she took a gentle pull, telling the theveing horse to go back. Again, Rosie did her best to co-operate but the shafts of the cart were stuck solid.

The little girl flipped herself around and leaning over the mare's fulsome bottom, unhooked the traces, next she unbuckled the breeching and belly band, leaving the straps hanging under Rosie's belly.

The teenager, who was somewhat restricted in her ability to give signals to the animal because her skinny legs were around the shafts and Rosie's ample belly, stood up on the ponies back and gracefully stepped onto the cart from where she gave the now relatively free pony a sound whack on the rump with a driving whip. The beast shot forward leaving the cart still firmly in the doorway and the shopkeeper in shock.

No one noticed the little girl leave nor was she known by any of the onlookers. I thought it quite remarkable that a modern thirteen year old girl could show more common sense and courage than any of the rubber necks gathered around.

The outcome of this fiasco was that the vehicle required extensive repairs; the shop required some refurbishing and the green grocer needed the help of a councillor. Rosie continued to go about her daily business and Rocking Boots contentedly puffed on his pipe and searched in his beard for intruders.

Helen and the Novelist
Chapter 17

    The big, bay gelding was on his toes from the moment he left his stable. He skittered about the yard, snapping and kicking at his rider as she tried, unsuccessfully, to vault into the saddle. Helen, positioned as she was, between the vicious teeth and the horse's cow kicking back leg, was at a bit of a disadvantage. On the third attempt, however, she made it into the saddle and quickly jamming her feet into the stirrups, gathered up the reins and joined the horses and riders now circling the stable yard with long elegant strides.

    The gelding was known to be a troublesome animal. With his impeccably breeding, outstanding conformation and on the form of his ancestors, he should have won good races, but his foul temper had caused so many problems on the racetrack that he was eventually withdrawn from racing and donated to the British Racing School in Newmarket, where he continued to make a nuisance of himself by bullying the young, hopeful students.

    I had known Helen since she was eight years old, she was such a tiny little thing back then, not that she is very big now. On a fine Saturday morning, she had wandered into my yard with her mum, Mary, and immediately began to make herself useful. By Sunday evening, she was an indispensable part of the fixtures and fittings. Helen was the sort of person that people and animals instinctively liked. It was not just because she was petite and pretty, she had a calming effect on people and horses.

Helen had her heart set on a career with horses, so it was inevitable that she should eventually want to spread her wings and further her knowledge and experience, and so, as soon as she was old enough she took herself off to Newmarket, the Mecca of the horse racing industry and enrolled at The British Racing School whose gain was my loss.

All riders were in the saddle now and receiving instruction from the trainers on how to ride each horse and what was expected of them on the gallops. It was a grand, fresh morning for riding and Helens mount, aptly named Bedevilled, was as usual, on the lookout for any opportunity to cause mayhem. He lunged at other horses with his teeth and kicked out at anything that got near him. His rider gave him a slap on the shoulder with her short racing whip to get his attention. Bedevilled responded by rearing high on his back legs almost unseating her but Helen was one step ahead of him and had a firm grip on his mane.

Eventually all the horses were on the move and settling into their work in a nice, orderly, active trot. As they reached the gallops Helen began to relax and enjoy her ride on the now unusually obedient Bedevilled. When the order came to canter. Bedevilled didn't need asking twice. He shot forward like an arrow from a bow and after a few strides was pulling a double handful. Helen bridged her reins in an attempt to hold him steady, and for a few strides the gelding allowed himself to be controlled. Gradually, the pace increased, Helen was now using all her strength to hold the galloping horse together. As the strength in her arms began to give out she knew that she was fighting a loosing battle that she stood no chance of winning. Bedevilled felt the girl tiring and took advantage of the situation. He threw his head up just missing smashing his poll into Helens face. Then pulled downwards pulling the reins from the girls hands and put in a series of fierce, stiff legged bucks ,throwing Helen over his head and under his steel shod hooves. To this day Helen can't remember much of what happened after hitting the ground but apparently she was kicked in the face resulting in two years of painful, re-constructive dental surgery and an end of her racing career. This would have discouraged, to say the least, a lesser person, but not our Helen. She was back in the saddle in no time, schooling show jumpers, helping on a stud farm and acting as a test pilot for me. What a girl, or was she just mad.

Every horse has its person, and as my old Dad use to say, "The trouble with horses is people". How right he was. Most horse owners are sound enough, if a little crazy, others are horse slaves who work hard, spend plenty and ride not at all. Renouncing any form of social life, they are happy to don welly`s and smelly anoraks seven days a week in the service of their ungrateful, long faced hay burner.

Judging at the Lusitano show 2006

On a grey, wet day in March 2000, I received a call from one such lady in Oldham. The towns name is derived from Owls Domain and until recently, the owl featured on all of the council's official documents until some fool suggested that it was politically incorrect to do so.

Yet Oldham has a lot going for it, a fine, modern theatre and theatre workshop that has turned out many famous actors. Oldham can also boast once having non other than Sir Winston Churchill as its M.P. So why, when entering the town under what I assume passes for a triumphal arch but is in reality a rusting railway bridge, are we greeted with the legend "Welcome to Oldham, home of the tubular bandage"? Surly Oldham has more to offer than that.

The land around Oldham is as confusing as the town. No flat fields to cultivate, just tortured mounds of rocky earth and black, dry stonewalls. I have heard it said that the ice age glaziers came roaring across the Pennines, saw Oldham and panicked, twisting every which way in an attempt to escape, causing the strange landscape in such places as Watershedings.

However, back to the phone call in March. The woman spoke or rather shouted, "Ah thee torse whispery"? "No" I replied. What a silly self-awarded title that is. I quietly explained to her what it was that I did do. This, alas ,encouraged her to explain in her own sweet way that "t' bloody 'orse is trying for t' bloody killt me" I said something like "Oh dear" not very helpful I know but I was thinking much worse. Desperate to get her off the phone ,I foolishly promised to go and see the horse next day and thought it would be a good idea to take Helen as moral and perhaps, physical support.

I have seldom been in a more depressing place. The dirt dark, stonewalls of the tightly packed buildings were running with water and slime, as though sweating and an unpleasant smell clung to everything. A shipen, converted into six small stables, housed six big horses. While a single bare light bulb, swinging on a highly suspect length of wire, attempted, unsuccessfully, to illuminate the entire stable block. The place was Dickensian at its worst. Helen had gone a decidedly unusual colour and ran out of this hell hole to find some fresh air.

From out of the gloom, a well rounded, wild looking person appeared as if by magic of the worst kind. Her dyed, blond hair was long, dirty and uncontrolled and she peered at me through little piggy eyes. She gave me a smile, I think, showing off what looked like wooden teeth. She was dressed in huge, dirty jodhpurs and a torn anorak that had once been black and white. I think she probably had hairy fetlocks hidden down her welly`s. I resisted the almost overwhelming desire to run away when the awful stench of her clothes nearly knocked me over.

"Wait thear" she told me, and I did as I was told, which was a novel experience for me. Eventually a piebald cob was led out into the muddy mess that passed for a yard. Surprisingly, he was a stunning animal and much cleaner than his owner was, although he still had that awful stench about him. He stood at about 15 hands to the withers with a white mane and a wealth of white feathering at his heels. His tail, tied up in an old Tesco bag to keep it out of the mud, swished angrily and he rolled his eyes as his fearsome owner directed a barrage of abuse at the top of her voice towards the unfortunate animal. I politely asked this epitome of womanhood what problems had she encountered with her horse. Her reply was classic.. "T bloody orse knows nowt and I'm a novelist". Oh dear. The lady then asked me how much it would cost to have the horse schooled "and I can pay thee bugger all till`t social pays mi benefits". I tried to price myself out of the job but she was most insistent that I take him . "t brass is no object". She said proudly, "thas`l just av to wait a bit si thee". She must have been on every state hand out in the book. Fortunately, she sold the horse before I allowed myself to be pressed into taking it on, thereby saving me and no doubt the poor horse a lot of grief.

That summer of 2000 was a very busy time, with horses coming to me for backing, schooling and rehabilitating after injuries. I have always found it less traumatic training driving horses than saddle horses, they seem to find it a little easier once they get use to the noise of the wheels and swindle trees. I always used an open bridle, that is a bridle without blinkers. I feel that horses are a lot happier if they can see what's going on, No doubt the purists will disagree.

In the spring of 2000, one of my regulars sent a stunning young horse along to be backed and schooled. As it stepped down from the trailer both Helen and I gazed at the horse in admiration, "wow" said Helen, I said nothing, The horse was an Anglo Arab mare with a deep mahogany colouring and great presence. She floated down the yard with a long free striding, confident walk. Helen walked around to the animals near side . "Oh my God" she cried " its blind" , Alarmed , I hurried to her side and sure enough where the horses left eye should have been was a great hole. Poor soul, I thought. The horses owner told me of the events leading up to the animals loss of its eye. It seems that it had been kicked in the head by a jealous mare resulting in surgery to remove the eye. She coped amazingly well and apart from carrying her head a little to one side to help her forward vision. The mare had adapted well to her disability.

We started the one eyed mares schooling in the usual way with a little lunging, only for five or ten minutes each day, Lunging can cause a lot of damage to a young horses joints and great care must be taken not to be too demanding, keeping the circles large to avoid over taxing the joints of the hind legs. We taught her to move away from pressure of the hand on her flanks to prepair her for riders leg sinals. On her blind side she had to learn to respond to the voice only, this was achieved by getting Helen to lead her around in circles on the lunge, the girl must have walked miles in the course of the mares education but eventually the horse was quite happy to walk and trot to voice commands. We always made our presence known when approaching her on her blind side, either by calling her name or talking nonsense to her as you would a driving horse in blinkers, a sudden pat on the rump could have resulted in one getting a good kicking. She was backed from the off side to let her see what was going on and she offered no resistance at all. If she humped her back a little when Helen squeezed with her legs, it was quite understandable and forgiveable. In common with many young horses she was taken by surprise when her rider went into a rising trot and she stopped dead, again, in time, she got use to it. The mare did so well that she became a very reliable hack and was quite happy to pop over a small fence. This little one eyed horse now had a happy future thanks to Helens hard work and skill.

Eventually, Helen bought her own horse, a nice little three year old, bright bay, Arab gelding named Pashka. That he had a rather grumpy disposition bothered Helen not at all and before long she was hacking Pashka out and about accompanied by her friend Rosie on her volatile, dun gelding, Brandy. I never expected the girls to return to the stables in one piece but they always did, occasionally they were followed by irate motorists who wanted payment for a wing mirror or paint work repairs to their cars but by and large they were unscathed by their adventures although Rosie had a few bumps due to Brandy playing at `wall of death` around the school as he swept the air with his tail and stepped sideways from under her, but the girl always came back with a smile and a curse.

An interesting horse arrived in the late summer of that year. It was a bright bay, trotting mare, I can`t recall her name, she had been involved in an accident on the track resulting in her loosing her confidence. The little mare was sold on as a riding horse although the poor soul had never been ridden in her life and it was all very strange to her. After years of having her head strapped up high she was now expected to keep it down. Like all horses of her breed she was built `down hill`, that is with most of her weight on her forehand, rather low in the stifle with a straight back leg. It seemed to me that it would be very unfair to expect this horse to be anything more than a Sunday morning hack, something to dobb around the lanes on, but alas her new owner had great plans for her mare and it took a lot to persuade her to modify her ambitions.

The mare was no trouble to back, but nothing would persuade her to listen to her riders legs,. This leg thing was quite alien to her as she had been taught to ignore the banging of shafts on her sides and so ignored the riders leg requests. Nor did she have any intention of going onto the bit. All her life she had had her head pulled up to allow her to use the muscles on the underside of her neck, unfortunately this caused her to force her chest down and her back to become rigid. All contrary to the desired rounded shape of a riding horse. Of course cantering was out of the question, she had neither the shape nor the inclination to do so and presumably had been discouraged from cantering in her early training.

All in all she had been a disappointment to both Helen and I. The mare went back to her owner not much better than she was when she had come to me and I hadn`t the heart to charge her a fee. I often see the lady hacking the little mare around the lanes, I think the horse has a happy home for life.

The most gentle horse we worked with was a black gelding named Harley, I still can`t decide whether he is Clydesdale or a Shire. He has the looks of a shire but the long striding walk of a Clydesdale. What a sensible and honest horse he was, and his owner, Aimee, had bonded well with him. Harley took to being a riding horse with no effort. No matter what was going on around him, he would take no notice and got on with his schooling. initially he had a big shambling, unbalanced baby trot, he wasn't aware of his hind legs until he was asked to trot over a pole, it shocked him to find that they didn't automatically bend to go over the pole but that he had to make some sort of effort, which he did in a most exaggerated way. The three joints in his back legs, the fetlock, hock and stifle, closed dramatically during every stride, so much so that we had to call a halt to the exercise for fear of putting too much strain on his young joints. Harley has a long way to go before he is ready for his first dressage test but I am sure he will do well in time and Aimee is so very patient and that is a big plus.

So often a horse gets a bad reputation through no fault of its own. Such a horse was Ben, a big, bay, Dutch warm-blood, he was full of his own importance. Ben had not been gelded long when his now owner Diane took him on and would spend a lot of time on his tip toes screaming at mares, unaware of anything other than the object of his desire. This made him a scary animal to handle. His primeval shouts seemed to shake the earth and vibrate through your bones. By the time Diane called me in to help, the `experts` had almost convinced her that the horse was mad, bad and dangerous and that she should get rid of him, or better still shoot him. My first impression on meeting him was of a good looking horse, in good health but a little noisy. I liked him and as we tacked him up for lunging I asked all the usual questions about his feeding, exercise routine and what was known of his past, this last question was met by a stony silence. I would have to take him at

My nice Jessica Bradshaw riding Olly at Broadway hunter trails 2006

face value. We walked him into the manage and allowed him a long rein, I wanted to see how he moved and carried himself without having to adapt to a small circle. The horse exploded in a fit of bucking and wind breaking until he shot off in a gallop, he took some holding that day and I almost lost him a few times, however, as soon as I had attached the side reins loosely to his bit, Ben went into a most beautiful shape and behaved splendidly. Someone must have spent a lot of time on this mysterious horse. Bit by bit the hidden Ben began to reveal its self. He had a knowledge of advanced school work and could jump with care and style. It took many weeks to get Ben to the point where he could be safely ridden out and although he still had an eye for the ladies, he became much more of a gentleman than he had been. And who could ask for more.

Tony Dampier has been a proffesional horseman for fifty five years. His work with horses has taken him to many parts of the world. He served in the Household Cavalry and as the Remounts Officer in the Royal Omani Cavalry. His great interest is in classical riding, teaching and rehabilitating problem horses. Tony`s first book "Kingdom of the Workhorse" was a best seller. He is a regular contributor to the Classical Riding Club magazine and in demand to give lectures and demonstrations .

Tony Dampier lives in Bury, Lancashire, with his wife Barbara.